Your Thinking Is
Your Superpower

MARTINE BOLTON

Cover & illustrations by Emma Paxton
www.imagistic.co.uk.

Interior by Lyn Thurman
www.quietrebelbureau.com.

**Get your free workbook and guided meditations
at: www.sunshinedevelopment.co.uk**

"I LOVE this book! It expertly condenses the gold nuggets from just about every brilliant personal & spiritual development practice ever.

In the short time that you fly through fluidly-laid, super-power activating exercises, guzzling the buffet of indispensable, pre-digested wisdom, you'll finish this book with wings sprouting from your shoulders and rockets on your feet! Your brain will have had a priceless re-modelling, and you'll be virtually unrecognisable next time you look in the mirror because your self-image has changed.

The author's generous personality and humour shines through, making every chapter not just an 'ah-ha moment' but a giggle to read.

Now I'm going to get a copy for each of my kids, which makes me even more super-powered! It's a gem of a book that's made simple sense of the last millennium of evolutionary thinking.

Thanks Martine. You're a star!"

- **Tara Love Perry,** International Master Soul Reader, Angelic Healer, and author of *I Love You, Me – 7 Steps to Transformational Self-Love.*

"Martine's book is an accessible and easy read, packed with effective tools to help you generate your superpower thinking style."

- **Lee Pycroft,** Makeup Artist & Human Givens Psychotherapist.

"Decades of life's learning material & experience, decluttered & presented Marie Kondo style in one place for us to reference ♥.

A life detox in one book - keep only what brings you JOY!"

- **Jane Cooke,** Founder - Free Range Women in Business.

"It's a choice between fear and love. Choose love and you will be powerful beyond measure!". Blessings upon blessings for your exciting new book. I hope you sell a million copies (in the first year!)."

- **Robert Holden,** author of *Shift Happens!*

YOUR THINKING

IS YOUR

SUPERPOWER

Conquer your Kryptonite…
Supercharge your thinking…
Transform your world!

Martine Bolton

For Joe and Max.

Here lie the secrets to building a wonderful life...

everything I wish I'd known sooner!

Much love always, Mum xx

YOUR THINKING IS YOUR SUPERPOWER

CONTENTS

Introduction

Hello and welcome! Thank you for investing in this little book. I'm Martine, and I've been very fortunate to discover information that's been super-helpful to me in life (transformational, really). I've distilled it into this book because I know it could be super-helpful and transformational for other people too. You probably wouldn't have picked it up if something hadn't piqued your curiosity – maybe a sense that it would have something helpful or interesting to offer. I believe that our intuition's working for us all the time if we listen to it. So, well done for finding yourself here today, and I trust that you'll find exactly what you need within these pages!

Over the years I've shared chunks of this information with the people I've come into contact in my work as a corporate trainer/consultant, and private NLP practitioner/ hypnotherapist. With this book, I'm bringing together a large part of my learning all in one place. My aim is to help you and others who read the book to transform your lives, businesses, and who knows... maybe your communities and our world for the better.

These days I find that most people understand the power of the mind, and are familiar with concepts such as positive thinking, the law of attraction, a growth mindset and so on. However, many of us still struggle to consistently direct our thoughts, emotions, actions and behaviours along positive, constructive lines, in order to create the kind results and outcomes that we'd like in our lives.

This book, if read or studied with a clear mind, and when the principles are practised regularly, will enable you to do just that. So, I encourage you to read it when your mind is fresh and you're in a place where you feel comfortable, relaxed and won't be too distracted. If you'd like to take notes or highlight the bits you want to be sure to remember, that will help you to absorb the learning more fully; and what will really help it all to stick is when you begin to take action on it - playing with it and testing it out. So, do look out for the opportunities that life will present you with, to put it all into practice.

This book contains the understanding, knowledge and awareness that I wish I'd known from a younger age, and that I believe will be useful to many people. It may well challenge some of your thinking and beliefs in some ways. So, I would simply encourage you to read and explore with an open mind, play with the ideas and techniques, do the activities, and then once you've done all that, decide for yourself.

To the best of my knowledge, based on the reading, research and experimenting I've done over the years, and on the experiences that I've had, the information herein is true and where possible, scientific. Where a concept that I speak about hasn't been evidenced, I point out that that's the case, leaving you free to use your discernment and draw your own conclusions. Bear in mind that not all our beliefs – however strongly we feel them to be true – are proven, and we're all prone to faulty and erroneous thinking at times.

We are still getting to grips with our understanding about how life works and what's really going on. In time, some of the ideas discussed in this book may well develop, and new discoveries are likely to be made. What we believe and come to know in the decades to follow will move on in some regards. However, it's my understanding that the key, central ideas discussed here are true, timeless and unchanging.

This book has been written to help anyone who recognises that their thinking patterns and habits might not always be helping them, and who'd like to change that in order to improve their life, achieve their goals and become happier, healthier, more successful and/or more prosperous. It is not intended to be a substitute for therapy or counselling. Whilst the information here is likely to be helpful for those experiencing stress, anxiety and mild depression, those experiencing more severe mental health problems and conditions should always seek formal psychological support.

My hope is that the information in this book will make a significant, positive difference in your life, enabling you to live the life that you deserve.

When you've finished reading, if you have any feedback that might help improve the book for future editions, please email contact@sunshinedevelopment.co.uk with your comments.

With thanks and very best wishes,

"YOU ARE TODAY WHERE
YOUR THOUGHTS HAVE
BROUGHT YOU;
YOU WILL BE TOMORROW
WHERE YOUR THOUGHTS
TAKE YOU"

- JAMES ALLEN -

Chapter 1

LIFE IS LITERALLY WHAT WE MAKE IT

You may have heard it said (or sung) before that "Life's what you make it", but what does that really mean?

At one time, I assumed it just referred to a person's outlook and what they chose to do with the opportunities that came their way. Maybe that was all it was intended to mean by the person who first said or penned it. Now, however, I perceive a deeper and more literal meaning to the statement – that we, personally, make our lives what they are; that we create our experience of life through the thoughts that we think, the feelings that our thoughts generate, the things we say and do (and don't say and do), the choices and decisions that we make, and the situations and behaviours that we tolerate, and those that we change or walk away from.

Every outcome can be traced back in some way to our thinking – from the way that we see things to how we interpret them, to what we then decide to do.

What positive or successful outcomes or results from your life can you recall, for which you're able to remember some of the thoughts, feelings and actions that are likely to have contributed to your success?

What less-than-positive (or unsuccessful) outcomes from your life can you recall, for which you can remember some of the thoughts, feelings and actions that may have contributed to those outcomes?

Can you see how your thoughts, feelings and actions may have influenced those things?

Some of us are pro-active in our lives – thinking in advance about all the things we'd like to experience - what we'd like to have, do, be, achieve... where we'd like to go... who we'd like to meet, and so on, putting in place plans for all of these things. Others of us are more re-active in our lives – going with the flow, being less planned and more spontaneous, and allowing life to surprise us.

Whether you're the kind of person who makes things happen, allows things to happen or wonders what happened, you will probably accept the scientific principle of causality (or cause and effect) that's in operation in our world. We might not be responsible for everything that happens to us in life (particularly in childhood, when we're not making all the decisions for ourselves), but we are responsible for how we perceive and react to what happens to us and what we do as a consequence. This can make all the difference between a positive and negative experience of life.

"Life's what you make it" doesn't necessarily mean that we create every single situation in our lives. Some situations happen totally outside of our control and we aren't personally responsible for them. However, how we perceive and interpret things, how we feel about them and the actions we subsequently take in response to them determine the impact and outcome that we ultimately experience – and <u>that</u> we *are* responsible for.

Life IS what we make it – we just share the experience with many others and therefore, don't get to personally create and control every aspect.

HEAVEN AND HELL

It's likely that some people you know have a great life and experience something close to heaven on earth - some of the time at least. It's also likely that you've met people who seem to have a pretty awful life, experiencing something close to hell on earth. Probably most of us experience a mixture of highs and lows, with quite a lot of averageness in between. What is it that makes the difference? Could it be that some people are just luckier (or unluckier) than others?

The definition of the word luck, according to the Oxford English Dictionary, is, 'Success or failure apparently brought by chance rather than through one's own actions.' The 'apparently' bit is interesting because it references the idea that whilst something may seem that way, it isn't necessarily so.

All people, over the course of a lifetime, can expect to meet with some amazingly positive experiences and some rather difficult ones too. Sometimes, the difficult ones aren't always happening to us personally, but to someone very close to us, and this has a knock-on effect.

Whilst I don't believe that we personally create every bad thing that happens in our lives, I do believe that we have a choice in how we think, feel and respond to those things. Some people experience and process a difficult life event relatively quickly and constructively, returning to normal functioning soon afterwards with no lasting loss of positivity. Others seem to get stuck in the negative emotions for long, drawn-out periods, struggling to bounce back, and maybe never quite recovering from what happened.

Heaven or hell, then, is subjective and not so much about what happens to us as it is about how we perceive and respond to what happens.

WHAT IS THINKING, WHERE DOES IT COME FROM, AND WHAT IS ITS PURPOSE?

Information, or data, comes to us from the world around us through our senses (what we can see, hear, touch, smell and taste). Thinking is an activity of the mind and brain where we consider, process and make sense of this information – often referencing past ideas, associations and memories in order to reach a conclusion or make a decision.

Unless we're in a coma or some form of vegetative state, we need to be able to think in order to survive. If we couldn't take in information, assess it quickly and come to a decision, we would most likely perish in early childhood. Basic survival aside though, we also need to be able to make sense of, and navigate, life, work, other people and everything else if we want to live good, happy and rewarding lives – which I'm going to assume that you do (*please note that assumptions are generally dodgy - some perhaps more so than others! They are mentioned in more depth in later chapters*).

We don't yet know everything there is to know about the mind and consciousness, and theories and models vary substantially, albeit with some commonalities. Sigmund Freud's iceberg model illustrated three different levels of mind - the conscious, subconscious and unconscious. Western philosophies point to multiple layers of mind (anywhere between three and seven of them) including higher, more spiritual aspects. It's important to remember that models are often just visual representations of how something is believed to be, rather than an accurate depiction of how something actually is. Statistician George Box once said, "Essentially, all models are wrong, but some are useful."

Personally, the Indian tradition that speaks of the three levels of conscious, subconscious and superconscious mind feels about right to me. The model and explanation to follow describe the levels as being arranged in a particular hierarchy, which might not be accurate. Other models depict them as being like layers of an onion. In reality it's probably not linear, but the model gives the general gist:

- The **superconscious** level, shown at the top here, is said to be where we're said to be connected to one another and to infinite intelligence (some call it the universal mind).
- The **conscious** level, shown in the middle, is said to be where we do most of our day-to-day thinking.
- The **subconscious** level, shown at the bottom, is said to be where our deeper memories, beliefs, values and so on are stored (our habits and auto-pilot responses come from the subconscious level).

The concept of a spiritual side to life (as referenced in the superconscious level) seems to be quite widely discussed and accepted these days – not just in religious environments but also in the context of holistic well-being, with the trinity of body, mind and spirit (or soul) and the idea that the world we operate in includes:

- The **physical** or material world that we can see, hear, feel, smell and touch;
- The **mental** world that is the realm of thought and mind-stuff;
- An unseen **spiritual** world, about which less is understood but that's been said to be the realm of the soul (the bit that animates us), and some might also say God and other non-physical beings. I don't think a spiritual aspect to life has been scientifically evidenced to date, or even if it would be possible to do so, assuming that one really exists.

All three aspects of body, mind and spirit are said to be linked, with each aspect impacting the others.

The subconscious aspect of our mind can and does influence our feelings and actions, but the conscious aspect is like the managing director. Many of us don't consciously direct our minds along positive, constructive lines, and therefore allow our thinking to go where it wants to go, unchecked. Some of us are also guilty of overthinking, relying solely on our conscious minds to come up with answers and solutions, when it can often be better to pose a question to the higher aspects of our superconscious (or universal) mind, where higher wisdom and intelligence are said to be accessible.

The quality of our thinking is foundational to the quality of our lives – in fact, you could say that thought is the material that constructs our lives, and that what we think about, we bring about. Probably the biggest difference between the highly successful people of our time (think of those with the kind of standing that Oprah Winfrey or Sir Richard Branson share), and the homeless person living under the bridge, is in the quality and content of the thinking that goes on between their ears. Their actions are important too of course, but all actions, behaviours and habits are traceable back through our feelings to our thoughts.

'Thinking' can constitute all or some of the following:

- Our day-to-day mental processing. The inner dialogue and mental imagery we generate. The opinions we hold, assumptions and judgements we make, and the biases we develop
- The concepts we hold about how things are - our metaphysical 'map of the world'
- Our beliefs about ourselves, other people, life, the universe and everything
- Our values - what's most important to us, and what isn't
- Our attitudes - the stance or position we take towards matters, people, things, etc.
- Our mindset (whether we work hard, or do as little as we can get away with; whether we 'know it all', or are open to new learning; whether we're grateful for everything, or take everything for granted; and so on).

From the moment we're born we are 'programmed' with fixed ideas that we get from other people and the environment around us, and that - as children at least - we tend to accept as truths. We also reach conclusions, based on our own experiences, that can be faulty. Maybe we have one or two bad experiences and from these, we create a generalised belief about the subject of the experience that isn't universally true.

Different people experience different ideas, environments and encounters, meaning that we all hold some opposite and conflicting concepts and beliefs, as well as some matching ones.

If we hold too tightly to the belief that our programming is correct and that other people's programming must therefore be wrong, this can get in the way of peaceful, harmonious living and create negative experiences and outcomes. Imagine for a moment that you were born in a different time, to a different set of parents, within a different gendered body, in another part of the world. Some of the ideas and beliefs you hold true today might well be very different. Much of what we think we 'know' to be true is faulty, or at least limited in its truth, so it serves us well to keep an open mind about most things.

IT'S GOOD TO KEEP AN OPEN MIND, BUT NOT SO OPEN THAT YOUR BRAIN FALLS OUT...

Our thinking, or mental processing, is the first step in the process that brings about the results and outcomes we experience. Our lives can be loosely divided up into the following areas:

Our results (or levels of contentment, happiness, success, etc.) in these areas are strongly reflective of the thoughts and beliefs we hold about them. Hold constructive thoughts and beliefs about a particular area of your life and you are likely to be happy and successful there; hold faulty or negative thoughts and beliefs in an area and you are likely to experience problems there, or at least be less happy and successful than you otherwise would be.

Take a moment now to consider how satisfied you are in each of these areas of your life on a scale of 1-10 (10 being the most satisfied) and mark the diagram in the appropriate places. You could shade/colour in the numbers up to your scores or simply draw a line across each segment at the relevant marks. We'll come back to this exercise later in the book.

OUR THOUGHTS CREATE OUR REALITY

The idea that our thoughts and minds have creative power in our lives has been around for thousands of years, having been suggested in scripts even pre-dating Christ, by individuals such as Lao Tzu, Buddha and others.

Many people today (possibly influenced by the explosion of 'New Thought' literature that's been published in the last century or so) believe that the inner world of mind and thought has an influence on the outer world – perhaps even preceding and creating it.

The study of quantum mechanics - also known as quantum physics and quantum theory - has demonstrated that everything in our universe is comprised, at the subatomic level, of vibrating particles of energy which respond to our consciousness. The 'observer effect' has shown that the mere observation of something is enough to change it.

The idea that the world isn't quite what it appears to be, and that the energy that everything consists of responds to our consciousness, can be mind-blowing. Many of us (myself included) struggle to get our heads around the concepts of quantum physics, and to be fair, we probably don't need to understand the concepts in too much detail for the information to be useful to us.

What it demonstrates is that the world that we perceive isn't necessarily how things really are and that our thinking influences what happens. The possibilities within this information are endless, as it suggests that by changing our consciousness (our thoughts, feelings, and therefore the energy, frequency and vibration that we generate) we can potentially change our experience.

THE T-F-A-R MODEL – FROM THOUGHTS TO RESULTS

The T-F-A-R model, popular in Cognitive Behavioural Therapy (CBT) and Neuro-Linguistic Programming (NLP), illustrates the relationship between our thoughts and the outcomes or results we achieve, in a more down-to-earth way:

THOUGHTS > FEELINGS > ACTIONS > RESULTS

In short, this means that our thoughts generate our feelings, which drive our actions, which create our results. Whilst this is a somewhat simplified version of what's quite a complex neurological, physiological and behavioural process, it's useful, nonetheless. The explanation to follow offers a bit more detail:

THOUGHTS

Every thought we think, every idea we accept, every belief we take on board, every concept we hold, every opinion we reach, every assumption or judgement we make, is being received and felt by our bodies at the physical level. Different kinds of thought have a different impact on the body depending on the energy vibration they produce (this is quantum physics and psychoneuroimmunology – not 'woo-woo'!). Depending on the nature of the thought, this impact can be either positive and enabling, or negative and disabling, and can contribute towards well-being and success, or ill-being and failure. For instance, if we believe we can do something, the chances are that we will feel confident and able, and probably complete the task successfully. Similarly, if we think we can't do something, the chances are that we will feel fearful and unable, and either avoid trying it, or try it but prove ourselves right and fail at the task. The belief becomes a self-fulfilling prophecy.

Additionally, a person who believes themselves to be a strong and healthy individual with a robust immune system will tend to experience less illness than someone who believes that they're less strong and healthy, and feels paranoid at the slightest sign that someone in their vicinity has a cold.

So, our thoughts are experienced by our physical bodies in the form of feelings, and all thoughts have power – either positive or negative. Whilst some people talk about neutral thoughts, there is probably no such thing. All of our thoughts have an impact, whether positive or negative.

FEELINGS

Whilst thoughts are the foundation of the results that we get, they can't, by themselves, create anything. However, our thoughts generate waves of emotion (the word emotion means energy in motion) which are then translated into feelings - some examples being frustration, delight and confidence.

Positive feelings such as love and happiness generate 'happy' hormones and chemicals in the body, which drive positive actions and behaviours, and are beneficial to our cells. Negative feelings such as anger, fear, stress and sadness generate a different set of hormones and chemicals in the body, which drive negative actions and behaviours and, if experienced intensely for prolonged periods of time, can be damaging to our cells.

Positive emotions drive positive actions, and negative or fearful emotions drive negative actions. If the feeling behind your actions is loving, you will tend to get a positive outcome. If the feeling is angry or fearful, you're unlikely to get a positive outcome. Maintaining positive thoughts and emotions in life is important, both for our health and for the outcomes we want to achieve.

Also, the body's response to emotions like stress and excitement is very similar – it's our thoughts that make an experience subjective. Therefore, different people can interpret the same event in very different ways. Our thoughts generate our feelings, and it's how we process and perceive an event that determines how we feel about it.

ACTIONS

A thought combined with a feeling is unlikely to have too much impact unless it's followed by an action or decision. Actions include the things we say and do, and our behaviours (how we say and do them); all of the little choices that we make, moment-by-moment; the bigger decisions that we take, including the decision not to do anything; our habits; and essentially anything that we do in response or reaction to a situation. Technically, it's our actions that bring about our results, although these wouldn't exist without the thoughts and feelings that drive them.

RESULTS

Every result in our lives is traceable back, through our actions and feelings, to a thought or mental pattern that we've held. So, if we want to achieve great results or positive outcomes (and I'm going to make the assumption that you do!), we need to become very conscious of our thoughts and feelings, and direct these along positive, constructive (even loving) lines that consider the greater good of all concerned. I speak more about the 'greater good' later in the book.

THE POWER OF THE MIND

There are many examples of the power of the mind in everyday life. For example:

- The Placebo Effect, where individuals experience relief from medical symptoms after taking a 'drug' that's really just a sugar pill
- The faithful devotees who experience spontaneous healings at Lourdes (and other sacred sites) every year
- The people who cure themselves of cancer through visualisation, meditation and similar practices
- The healthy individuals who've died after being told they would soon do so by witch doctors, and the like
- Those who can control their body temperature, heart rate, etc. using biofeedback techniques
- Those who use visualisation for improvement in sports performance

- The use of hypnosis to alleviate pain in childbirth, or as a substitute for anaesthesia in the operating theatre
- Those who've achieved feats of super-human strength, like lifting a car to free a child trapped underneath it following an accident
- British comedian (and non-athlete) Eddie Izzard completing 27 marathons in 27 days to raise money for the charity Sport Relief, and others who've achieved similar 'improbable' feats.

As Henry Ford is quoted to have said, "Whether you think you can do a thing or think you can't do a thing, you're right." Maybe there's nothing we can't achieve when we hold a vision and believe it's possible.

THE LAW OF ATTRACTION

The law of attraction (one of a set of 'universal laws' said to have first been documented within the Emerald Tablets of Hermes Trismegistus) is the name given to the principle of like attracting like. In the context of this book, this means that positive thoughts, feelings and actions tend to create positive results or outcomes, and negative thoughts, feelings and actions tend to create negative results or outcomes. In this way, our thoughts create our reality.

The New Thought Movement of the mid-late 1800s and early 1900s inspired a glut of literature on subjects like the law of attraction, metaphysics, mind/body healing, positive thinking and visualization, that's continued to the present day. Rhonda

Byrne's bestselling book, *The Secret*, published in 2006, brought the concept of the law of attraction to the mainstream, hence many people today are at least aware of it – even if they don't understand it or believe it to be real.

It's probably fair to say that this law has been somewhat misrepresented in recent times – often being portrayed as an easy way to get hold of all the material things you want in life just by thinking about them and believing they are yours. Whilst this is no doubt a part of it, it's not just the thought that counts – it's also the feelings we generate and the actions we take (and don't take) that make the difference.

In my personal experience, things don't often materialise straight away as soon as we start thinking about them (although I have had a few surprising experiences). Often, they take hard work and persistence over a longer period. To quote a Japanese proverb, 'Vision without action is just a daydream.'

I personally tend to speak in terms of 'the creative power of thought' or 'the power of the mind' instead of the law of attraction, but only because the law has been so misunderstood.

CHAPTER 1 SUMMARY

✓ Our lives are literally what we make them with our thoughts, feelings and actions. We might not be personally responsible for creating all of the circumstances of our lives (after all, we share our world with many other people who are also creating stuff with their thoughts), but we are responsible for how we respond to life's circumstances, and for the outcomes we subsequently get.

✓ Thinking is the mental processing that we do to make sense of what's happening and decide what action (if any) we need to take. It's necessary for our survival and is therefore a helpful process, but sometimes we can overthink things - over-relying on the conscious part of our minds and under-utilising the deeper parts where higher wisdom and intelligence are said to be accessible.

✓ Our thoughts create our feelings, which drive our actions and behaviours, which create the outcome or results that we get. If we can choose thoughts and generate feelings that come from a positive, constructive, loving place that takes everyone's best interests into account, things are more likely to turn out well for us. All other kinds of thinking, for example selfish and negative thoughts, work against us, and are ultimately self-defeating.

✓ Our minds are extremely powerful. With our thoughts we can think and feel ourselves into wellness, illness and into doing and achieving absolutely anything. Just imagine the possibilities! It's crucial, therefore, that we direct our thoughts and feelings in positive, constructive ways as much as possible to ensure that we're creating the kind of outcomes that we do want and not those that we don't want.

✓ Our experience of life can feel like heaven or hell. We always have a choice in what we focus on and how we subsequently feel. Some events in life are tragic or very difficult, and, of course, we do need to process and work through our feelings. However, if we continue to focus intently on the hardship, loss or tragedy of a situation long after it's passed instead of rebuilding our lives and feeling grateful for our many blessings, we can cause ourselves a lot of unnecessary suffering.

✓ The law of attraction, like the law of gravity, is a universal law that has always been in place. It has suffered from misrepresentation in recent years, but it essentially means that what we think, how we feel and what we do creates every outcome in our lives. If we're not entirely happy with an aspect of our lives, all we need to do is change how we're thinking and feeling about it, and do something different to what we have been doing, and we'll get a different result. And that's the basis of this book!

"YOU MUST UNLEARN
WHAT YOU HAVE BEEN
PROGRAMMED TO
BELIEVE SINCE BIRTH.
THAT SOFTWARE NO
LONGER SERVES YOU IF
YOU WANT TO LIVE IN A
WORLD WHERE ALL
THINGS ARE POSSIBLE"

- JACQUELINE PURCELL-

Chapter 2

WE'VE BEEN PROGRAMMED

From the moment we're born (and some may argue, beforehand), our minds are effectively being programmed, like a computer, by everything we experience.

If, when we are small, we are held, loved and all our needs are met, we learn that we are safe, that life is good and so are we. If the faces around us are open, relaxed and happy, and if the voices and sounds we hear are upbeat and joyful, we learn that life is a fun and pleasant experience. If we're told from an early age that we're wonderful, talented and unlimited, our minds accept this as true. If we're taught that other people are similarly wonderful and that when we co-operate and collaborate, we can achieve anything, that's how we'll operate. If we're taught that life is a wonderful adventure in learning, developing and creatively shaping and advancing the world we live in, then that's what we'll make it.

I don't think anyone has the perfect upbringing, although some probably come close. We all receive at least a bit of negative input from the world around us that can have the effect of making us feel unsafe, or can cause us to question our capability or value. Sadly, some people experience a terrible early life where they are constantly put down, abused, and almost all the messages they receive are negative. Most of us probably experience something in between these two extremes. I do believe, though, that if most of us were more conscious of the ways in which we raise and nurture our children, and the beliefs we imprint upon them, we could collectively create a much better experience of life for everyone. This world we live in is largely what we humans have made it, and we can unmake and remake it as we wish.

In computing, the GIGO principle (garbage in, garbage out) tells us that the quality of the output reflects the quality of the input – i.e. the programming that's been received. It doesn't matter whether a computer is programmed with faulty or factual input data – it simply accepts its programming as correct, and makes all its calculations on that basis. It's the same with humans, where particularly as children, we tend to accept what we hear, what we see and what we conclude, without question.

If we're working with flawed input data, our output will be compromised, manifesting in problems and unsatisfactory outcomes. If we're working with sound input data, we're likely to find that everything flows smoothly, and we get excellent outcomes. That's not to say that we should bring our children up to believe that life is always going to be wonderful, and that they themselves are perfect in every way. We can be positive without being delusional! It's just that we should equip them with the kind of mindset and thinking skills they'll need to solve the problems and challenges they'll face in life, and to reflect and work on themselves when required.

BELIEFS

Our beliefs can come from many sources including what we're told by other people, what we read or see portrayed in the media and the conclusions we make based on our experiences and what we notice about the world around us. They are extremely powerful because what we believe tends to become true for us, regardless of whether it has any basis in 'fact' - as is the case with the self-fulfilling prophecy.

Beliefs can be about ourselves (our personality, our traits, our strengths and weaknesses; what we can and can't do; what we're worth; what we do and don't deserve; whether we're lucky or unlucky); about other people generally; about specific kinds of people; about relationships; love; religious or spiritual beliefs; political beliefs; beliefs about life; the world; work; money; our health, weight, appearance; what's important and not important, and just about anything else. We tend to hold on tightly to our beliefs and assume that they're right, when they're just thoughts and ideas that we've picked up somewhere and many are likely to be faulty, or at least limited in their truth. Here are some examples:

NEGATIVE/UNHELPFUL	POSITIVE/HELPFUL
Life's a bitch (and then you die)	Life's a beach
I am limited in what I can have, do and be	There's nothing I can't have, do and be
People can't be trusted	People are generally good
You've got to watch your back	Life has your back
There's not enough to go around	There's plenty for everyone

NEGATIVE/UNHELPFUL	POSITIVE/HELPFUL
There's never enough time	There's always time for what's most important
I'm never good enough	I'm always good enough
I'm better than others	No man is greater or lesser than another
My customers are a pain	My customers are a joy
You've got to compete and win	Together we achieve more
Things never turn out how I want them to	Things are always working out for me
Asking for help is a sign of weakness	It's ok to ask for help. People love helping
Happiness lies in the future	Today is the most important day there is
I'll be happy when I have (……….)	I already have everything I need
Bad things always happen to me	I learn from everything that happens to me
It's important that I impress others	It's important to do what makes me happy
I might fail, so I won't try	I will never regret giving something a try

The person in the left-hand column is going to have a life that largely reflects the beliefs listed there. The person in the right-hand column is going to have a life that largely reflects the beliefs listed there. There might be nothing in these columns that can be proven to be universally and objectively true, and yet for those that believe these things, they will almost certainly become self-fulfilling.

Expectations are also very powerful, and there are some interesting cases and stories relating to teachers' expectations of their students' performance. In one study by *Robert Rosenthal and Lenore Jacobsen* in 1968, researchers incorrectly told teachers that certain students (randomly selected) were potential high achievers, and were expected to bloom over the year ahead. When they went back at the end of the school year, they found that those students, and particularly the younger ones, had demonstrated greater intellectual development than the others.

Another study by researchers at Yale University followed middle-aged adults for twenty years. Those who held positive beliefs about aging lived an average of 7.6 years longer than those who held negative beliefs about aging.

My mother was a nurse, and for much of her career, she cared for elderly patients in hospitals and nursing homes. She was adamant that she didn't want to "make old bones" and would often say she'd be content with "three score years and 10". Sure enough, she happily passed away at the age of 70, feeling like she'd done her bit in life, and was ready to go.

The internal stories we tell ourselves about who we are, where we come from and where we're going can also be powerful and self-fulfilling. We probably all have an identity narrative describing certain characteristics (for example, "I'm Martine Bolton; personal development consultant; wife, mum, sister, daughter, aunty, friend; lover of long walks, adventures, sunshine, sunsets; tall-ish, slim-ish, white British female…" and so on). However, this identity is really very limited.

Our names are just labels that are used to identify us and

distinguish us from others. Our roles in life relate to what we do, and not who we are. Our physical features describe the bodies we were born into, not who we are inside those bodies. Our identities are usually past- or present-oriented, and say nothing about our potential, or who we are becoming. Who we think we are is quite limited - who we really are is much broader and more expansive than we realise.

Psychoanalyst Carl Jung's concept of archetypes (described as inborn tendencies toward certain classic behaviours or personality types) no doubt plays a part in our identity too. The 12 key archetypes are: The Innocent; The Sage; The Explorer; The Outlaw; The Magician; The Hero; The Lover; The Jester; The Everyman; The Caregiver; The Ruler; The Artist. Other archetypes have been described too, and there's plenty of information on the subject available freely online. We will all identify, at least in part, with one or more of the 12, and they can strongly influence how we think, feel and behave. However, we are much more than the 'types' that we identify with, and we can consciously choose to develop other aspects within ourselves at any time if our current behaviour doesn't always serve us well.

We may also have a life story that we tell ourselves and others, setting out the main plot of our lives – past, present and sometimes future. This is usually formed from the stand-out events (positive and negative) that we've experienced in life. Our stories aren't always entirely conscious, but it's useful to try and make them so because if they're not helping us, we can choose to change them and alter our future direction.

Our life stories may fit loosely into one or more of the following classic story themes including: Overcoming the Monster; Rags to

Riches; The Quest; Voyage and Return; Comedy; Tragedy; and Rebirth. They can feature good and evil heroes and villains, and have an overall theme of either triumph or disaster. Whilst they may be based around facts and events, they're not real because they are formed of selective bits of our lives (and the meaning we've given them) and are distorted by the bits we've left out.

So, our personalities and lives are, to a significant extent, an act of self-creation. If we're not 100% happy with who we think we are and where we think we're headed, we can re-write our stories and our roles and make them what we want.

Take some time out to consider the life story that you've been telling yourself and make some notes below:

In a nutshell, the story of my life from cradle to grave is:

_____

_____

_____

_____

_____

_____

_____

_____

_____

_____

It's also worth doing an inventory of your key beliefs – particularly regarding the positive beliefs that are likely to be serving you well, and any negative or limiting beliefs that may be causing problems or holding you back. Please make some notes in the spaces below:

I believe I am:

_____

_____

_____

_____

_____

_____

I believe I'm not:

_____

_____

_____

_____

_____

_____

_____

Other beliefs I hold about myself are:

_____

_____

_____

_____

_____

_____

_____

_____

_____

Beliefs I hold about other people in general include:

_____

_____

_____

_____

_____

_____

_____

_____

_____

Beliefs I hold about specific kinds, or groups, of people include:

_____

_____

_____

_____

_____

_____

_____

_____

Beliefs I hold about life, the world and the universe include:

_____

_____

_____

_____

_____

_____

_____

_____

_____

Beliefs I hold about friendship include:

_____

_____

_____

_____

_____

_____

_____

_____

Beliefs I hold about other relationships include:

_____

_____

_____

_____

_____

_____

_____

_____

Beliefs I hold about love include:

_____

_____

_____

_____

_____

_____

_____

_____

_____

Religious and spiritual beliefs I hold include:

_____

_____

_____

_____

_____

_____

_____

_____

_____

Beliefs I hold around money include:

_____

_____

_____

_____

_____

_____

_____

_____

_____

Beliefs I hold around my health and well-being include:

_____

_____

_____

_____

_____

_____

_____

_____

Beliefs I hold around my appearance and/or weight include:

_____

_____

_____

_____

_____

_____

_____

_____

Other beliefs that I suspect are having a beneficial or detrimental impact on my life include:

_____

_____

_____

_____

_____

_____

_____

_____

In the following chapter we'll review any beliefs you've uncovered that could be causing you problems, and consider whether there are any more helpful beliefs that you could embrace. For now, though, let's look at something else that can reflect our beliefs – and that's our attitudes.

ATTITUDES

An attitude is a way of thinking and feeling about something or someone that reflects our viewpoint, mindset, values and beliefs, and is displayed in our body language and tone of voice. Thoughts and feelings in general have a habit of leaking out in our behaviour, so when we're talking about negative or unhelpful attitudes, the wise person works to transform from the inside-out by upgrading their thoughts and feelings, rather than just masking their attitude or adjusting their behaviour.

Of course, there may be times when allowing our negative attitudes and feelings to be expressed can be helpful, but I feel this is best done very mindfully and respectfully, having considered the desired outcome and best time, place, etc. for the conversation.

Some examples of attitudes we can hold include:

- Believing that life owes us something without us having to do anything
- Believing that we're here to help others, and that we receive in proportion to what we give
- Being thankful for everything that comes our way

- Taking everything that comes our way for granted
- Feeling that we're better than; or not as good as; or equal to others
- Having a "Can do" or "Give it a go" attitude
- Having an "It can't be done" attitude
- Being cynical about everything
- Being enthusiastic about everything.

These are just a few examples. There are many more. The important thing to remember about attitudes is that other people can smell them! Our actions totally give them away, and our attitudes towards others can influence theirs towards us, as is demonstrated in the Betari Box model below:

The gist of the model is (1) my attitude affects my behaviour; (2) my behaviour influences your attitude towards me; (3) your attitude towards me affects your behaviour; (4) your behaviour towards me will reinforce what I already think of you.

How we perceive ourselves and others strongly influences the feel of our communication and the quality of our relationships. These 'perceptual positions' are illustrated brilliantly in the 'OK Corral' model by Franklin H. Ernst Jr. (adapted below), which represents the work of psychiatrist, and originator of Transactional Analysis, Dr. Eric Berne:

I am not OK **You are OK** One-down position Feels less worthy (Lose/Win)	**I am OK** **You are OK** Healthy position Feels equally worthy (Win/Win)
I am not OK **You are not OK** Hopeless position Feels equally unworthy (Lose/Lose)	**I am OK** **You are not OK** One-up position Feels more worthy (Win/Lose)

The term 'OK' in the model generally refers to the fundamental value we perceive in ourselves and others (Stewart and Joines, 1987).

In the top right-hand section, we have the "I'm OK: You are OK" position, where we are likely to perceive ourselves and the other person as having equal value and importance. When we approach an interaction or relationship from this attitude or position (and especially if the other person approaches the interaction from the same position too), it's highly likely that things will go smoothly, our interactions will feel good and positive, both parties will get their needs met, and the relationship will be good and strong. The other person will feel our good-will and send it back to us.

In the top left-hand section, we have the "I'm not OK: You are OK" position, where we perceive ourselves as not having as much value or importance as the other person. When we approach an interaction or relationship from this perspective (and especially if the other person approaches the interaction from the opposite position of perceiving that they have more value or importance than us), it's likely that the other person will get their needs met at our expense. They are likely to feel great, and we will either feel resigned to the outcome (because we believe they deserve it more), or we may feel unhappy, resentful, or similar.

In the bottom right-hand section, we have the "I'm OK: You're not OK" position, where we perceive ourselves as having more value or importance than the other person. When we approach an interaction or relationship from this perspective (and especially if the other person approaches the interaction from the opposite position of perceiving that they have less value or importance than us), it's likely that we will get our needs met at the other person's expense. This may feel great for us, but not so good for them, and will likely come at a cost to good-will in the relationship.

Finally, in the bottom left-hand section we have the "I'm not OK: You're not OK" position, where we perceive both ourselves and the other person as having little value or importance. It's difficult for any good to come out of this position for either party, with interactions typically getting nowhere and ending in dissatisfaction for both.

Whilst there might be situations where winning at the other party's expense, allowing the other party to win at your expense, or even ending a situation with both parties losing might be OK, generally speaking, the only basis for truly healthy relationships and happy outcomes is the "I'm OK: You're OK" position.

Information that I've been exposed to in my life has led me to believe that we all come from the same source (a religious/spiritual idea) and that we all have equal intrinsic value and worth (an idea that's probably traceable back to the US Declaration of Independence and Martin Luther King Jr's "I have a dream" speech). Whilst these beliefs feel like fundamental truths, I can't claim that they're facts. They would, however, suggest that fundamentally, everyone is OK, regardless of their behaviour.

It can be difficult to perceive someone as OK when they've committed terrible crimes or done something against you or someone you love. 'Good and worthy' relates to our essence – not necessarily our conduct. Personally, I don't believe anyone is born bad or evil. Our experiences shape us. Not having the love and nurture that we needed as babies and children shapes us. Abuse shapes us. Indoctrination shapes us. Sometimes brain damage and defects impact a person's behaviour. That doesn't mean that we should be soft on crime, criminals and people who behave badly – just that it's generally more effective to take a corrective, restorative approach than it is to take a punitive one, remembering that, at essence, we are all the same – good and worthy of respect. Difficult sometimes, I concede, but not impossible, and no doubt necessary if we want to create a better world... which I hope you do!

We are often taught to compete with, and compare ourselves with others, however, this is a recipe for unhappiness. We all have strengths and talents in different areas. There will always be someone better or worse than us at something. There will also always be someone cleverer, richer and better looking. Our ego (or sense of our 'self' as being separate to others) will often find ways of fooling us into thinking that we are more or less special than other people. We're not – we're all just different - differently talented, differently more or less able – but not greater or lesser in our essence.

So, we need to cultivate constructive attitudes about ourselves, other people and everything else. Unwholesome attitudes take us nowhere good. As author Denis Waitley said, "Your attitude is either the lock on, or the key to, the door of your success."

Reflect on some of the relationships you've had with people in the past and make a few notes on the positions you took and the outcomes they had:

Someone I liked and felt good around:

_____

_____

_____

_____

Someone I didn't feel as good as:

_____

_____

_____

_____

Someone I felt better than:

_____

_____

_____

_____

Someone I didn't like and felt bad around:

_____

_____

_____

_____

Are there any actions you could take to help you adopt a position of "I'm OK: You're OK" with more people, more of the time? If so, what are they?

_____

_____

_____

_____

_____

_____

_____

_____

MINDSET

The word 'mindset' describes a person or group's world view, based on a firmly established set of ideas and attitudes that determine how they respond to things. The most commonly known mindsets are probably positive and negative mindsets, followed close by fixed and growth mindsets, as described by Carol Dweck in her book *Mindset: The New Psychology of Success*, first published by Random House in 2006.

A positive mindset means focusing on the positive things in life, and instead of getting discouraged when faced with problems and challenges, looking at how we can overcome them. A negative mindset is the opposite – focusing on the negatives, on what might go wrong, and becoming bogged down in the problems and challenges so that we can't move beyond them into more resourceful thinking.

A fixed mindset is one where we believe that our intelligence, abilities and potential are fixed at birth, and that no matter what we do, we can't develop beyond our perceived set limits. A growth mindset is the opposite, where we believe that our intelligence, abilities and potential can be developed through effort and persistence. In the fixed world, talent is king; in the growth world, hard work wins out.

There are many other examples of mindset, including the follower mindset, where individuals look towards leaders to make decisions and tell them what to do; the short-term mindset, where individuals make choices based on what they want today rather than considering longer-term goals; and the poverty and millionaire mindsets, amongst others. But these are all just collections of ideas, beliefs, thoughts and attitudes, and they can potentially be changed and/or strengthened.

VALUES

Our personal values are the things we tend to hold most important and dear in our lives. We subconsciously consider these values when making most of our choices and decisions in life.

Many of us share similar values, although we may rank them in different orders of importance, depending on our age and stage in life. For example, many people would include Security, Love,

Health, Achievement and Happiness somewhere in their top 10 lists. When we're younger, Love, Achievement, Fun, Independence and Adventure, might be higher up our list rather than, say, Health, Security, Community, Companionship and Safety, which might become more important to us in the later stages of our lives. That's not to say that we don't want fun and adventure in our later years (some of us feel younger at heart with every passing year!) or that we don't want safety and a sense of community when we're young – just that for some of us, they might become a little more or less important at different times, depending on our circumstances.

Some of what we value relates to our inherent needs, but other values are programmed into us by our families, our religions - even by the media and other influences. For example, some of us are pushed to achieve academically as children. We may be strongly encouraged to pursue certain professions – often those that our parents will be proud of or that will provide us with a certain level of income – and these sometimes have very little to do with our passions and abilities. We can be hoodwinked into believing that Money, Status, Power and Popularity are what we should be chasing, and that if we don't have a big house, new car, the latest tech, branded clothing, expensive holidays, and so on, then we're not worth very much as a person.

So many of us try to add value to ourselves by buying expensive things, but all the 'bling' in the world can't buy self-esteem or happiness. None of that stuff really matters. Certainly, no thing or amount of money can bring us lasting happiness, or fill a sense of emptiness. Love, connection, contribution – these are the only kinds of things that can truly do that.

So, it's vital to get real about what's most important to you in your life – not what other people have said should be important to you, but the things that, when in place, will bring about lasting fulfilment. Once you know what these things are, you have a much greater chance of creating them in your life, and knowing them can also make decision-making more straight-forward.

Have a go at circling or highlighting the values that hold significance for you from the list to follow, then create a 'Top 10' list in order importance. If there are any values missing from the list for you, write these in the blank spaces at the bottom, and if you're prone to over-thinking these kinds of things, try to do it quickly. It may well change a little over the years anyway.

Authenticity	Friendships	Reputation
Achievement	Fun	Respect
Adventure	Growth	Responsibility
Authority	Happiness	Safety
Autonomy	Health	Security
Balance	Honesty	Self-Respect
Beauty	Humour	Service
Boldness	Influence	Spirituality
Compassion	Inner Harmony	Stability
Challenge	Justice	Success
Citizenship	Kindness	Status
Community	Knowledge	Trustworthiness
Competency	Leadership	Wealth
Contribution	Learning	Wisdom
Creativity	Love	Peace

Curiosity	Loyalty	Pleasure
Determination	Meaningful Work	Poise
Fairness	Money	Popularity
Faith	Openness	Recognition
Fame	Optimism	Religion

Now list your top ten circled or highlighted values in order of importance to you:

1. _____

2. _____

3. _____

4. _____

5. _____

6. _____

7. _____

8. _____

9. _____

10. _____

Look at these again and reflect on the questions to follow:

Why are these things so important to you?

_____

_____

_____

_____

_____

_____

_____

Are you sure they're your own values and not someone else's (i.e. your parents', society's, the media's, etc)?

_____

_____

_____

_____

_____

_____

_____

_____

What do you perceive valuing these things will bring to your life? For example, will they bring you genuine happiness and fulfilment? Are you sure?

_____

_____

_____

_____

_____

Pinpoint the things that are most important to your health and happiness, and you will have an excellent navigation tool for life that will make even the toughest decisions easier.

The final point to reflect on for this section is whether your life, as it stands currently, reflects the values that you've highlighted. If not fully, then what would need to change in order to bring your life into alignment with what's important to you, and what steps will you take towards these changes? Make some notes here:

_____

_____

_____

_____

_____

_____

CHAPTER 2 SUMMARY

✓ Like computers, our minds are effectively 'programmed' with thoughts and ideas. These tend to come from other people (particularly during our early years, when we're less likely to question and reject them), however, programming can happen all through our lives, and includes the conclusions we make, based on our experiences. Like the principle of GIGO (garbage in, garbage out), our results in life depend on the quality of those thoughts and ideas – some being more helpful to us than others.

✓ We adopt beliefs throughout our lives, and these can be thought of as our 'map of the world' – our understanding of the world we live in (who we are, what we're here for, what's important, and so on). Our beliefs are extremely powerful, and tend to be self-fulfilling. The world we experience is a projection of our dominant thoughts and illusions, which play out like scenes in a movie where we are the main character.

✓ Our attitudes convey our inner thinking and leak out in our body language and tone of voice, where other people pick up on them. This happens even if we think we're good at masking the negative ones.

✓ Our mindset determines just about everything in our lives, including how happy and healthy we'll be, and the levels of success and prosperity we'll experience.

✓ Our values shape all the choices and decisions we make in life, potentially leading to a life of happiness and fulfilment, or one of frustration and emptiness.

"THE STORY THAT YOU'RE LIVING IS THE STORY YOU KEEP TELLING YOURSELF, OVER AND OVER. START TELLING A BETTER FEELING STORY"

- ABRAHAM HICKS -

Chapter 3

WE CAN REPROGRAMME OURSELVES

We learned in the last chapter how everything we know is either an idea that we picked up from our environment, or a conclusion we made based on our experiences. We also learned that a significant proportion of this is likely to be limited in its truth, if not completely faulty. You may have identified some beliefs or attitudes that have been causing problems in your life. If that's the case, don't be too concerned, because they are only thoughts and ideas, and are not set in stone. We can simply choose to throw the faulty and unhelpful ones onto the metaphorical scrap heap, and choose to adopt some new, more helpful ones instead.

That said, some programming can be a bit persistent, and old thoughts, beliefs and feelings might re-surface from time to time. When this happens, it helps if we can learn to see them for what they are – simply shadows from the past, with no validity in the present. We can then just consciously let them go as soon as possible, and get on with whatever we were doing.

We can also choose to replace them with something more helpful, if liked. For example, we could visualise ourselves ceremoniously throwing the old thought, belief or feeling onto an imaginary scrap heap and saying something like, "Good riddance old thought/feeling... you're not real, and you're not helping me!" Then, we could visualise what we want instead (in relation to the situation that triggered the thoughts or feelings), and consider the kinds of thoughts and feelings we'll need to hold to make that happen. Just thinking of these will begin the process of change. The subconscious mind (and the body) always follow the directions of the conscious mind, and so we can choose to redirect ourselves as needed.

When we think a thought or hear a message enough times, it creates a neural pathway in the brain that strengthens and reinforces it until it becomes an ingrained belief, thinking habit or pattern. It's quite interesting that, from a biological point of view, the brain gets rid of old neural pathways periodically. These become weakened when we pay no attention to them, and eventually they disintegrate. We can establish new neural pathways by repeatedly thinking and speaking more helpful thoughts, beliefs and messages, and with a bit of time, these become our new thinking habits and patterns.

Whilst our brains are most malleable during childhood, neuroplasticity (where a brain reorganizes itself and forms new neural connections) continues throughout our lives.

RE-WRITING OUR PROGRAMMING

It's entirely possible to re-write our programming. However, it could be quite overwhelming to try and do a full inventory of all the thoughts, ideas, beliefs, attitudes, and so on that you've been programmed with and replace them all at the same time. Instead, you may wish to start by taking a look at one priority area of your life where you're not currently as happy and successful as you'd like to be (maybe referring back to the pie-chart activity in Chapter 1), and ask yourself the following scrutiny questions:

SCRUTINY QUESTIONS

What thoughts, ideas, beliefs, opinions, etc. do I hold around this part of my life?

Where did they come from?

How do I know these are true? Do other people believe different things? Why?

What evidence do I have that my beliefs are true?

What evidence might I find to the contrary (if I looked)?

What kinds of thoughts, ideas, beliefs, opinions, and so on, might the people who have great success in this area hold?

> **What if my past thinking has been faulty, and I'm open enough to consider a new reality?**
>
> **What outcomes might I create or achieve in the future?**
>
> **Am I willing and ready to change my mind today?**

If you're up for a bigger, more comprehensive exercise, you could try working through all or some of the questions to follow:

Who would I be without this programming, and in what ways might I be different? For example: would I be more successful... confident... happy, etc? Would my life flow more smoothly or with less drama?

_____

_____

_____

_____

_____

_____

What makes me happy and 'lights me up'?

_____

_____

_____

_____

_____

_____

_____

_____

If there was a purpose to my life, what is it? If there was a reason I chose to be here, now, having these experiences, what is it?

_____

_____

_____

_____

_____

_____

_____

_____

What do I want?

_____

_____

_____

_____

_____

_____

_____

_____

_____

What do I most hope to achieve before my life is over? What kind of legacy might I want to leave behind?

_____

_____

_____

_____

_____

_____

_____

_____

What would I like people to think, feel and say about me?

_____

_____

_____

_____

_____

_____

_____

_____

If I could re-write my narrative (or life story), how would I like it to go?

_____

_____

_____

_____

_____

_____

_____

_____

Flick back to the previous chapter to the section where you wrote down some of your current beliefs. Based on beliefs being self-fulfilling, what would some better, more helpful beliefs to hold (and that your mind doesn't completely reject) be? Think of the kind of beliefs that would bring about the outcomes or results that you'd like and make some notes in the spaces below:

Some better beliefs about myself that I'd prefer to hold include:

_____

_____

_____

_____

_____

Some better beliefs about people in general that I'd prefer to hold include:

_____

_____

_____

_____

_____

_____

Some better beliefs about specific kinds or groups of people that I'd prefer to hold include:

_____

_____

_____

_____

_____

Some better beliefs about life and the world or universe that I'd prefer to hold include:

_____

_____

_____

_____

_____

Some better beliefs about friendships that I'd prefer to hold include:

_____

_____

_____

_____

_____

Some better beliefs about other relationships that I'd prefer to hold include:

_____

_____

_____

_____

_____

_____

Some better beliefs about love that I'd prefer to hold include:

_____

_____

_____

_____

_____

Some better beliefs about religion and spirituality that I'd prefer to hold include:

_____

_____

_____

_____

_____

Some better beliefs about politics that I'd prefer to hold include:

_____

_____

_____

_____

_____

_____

Some better beliefs around work that I'd prefer to hold include:

_____

_____

_____

_____

_____

Some better beliefs around money that I'd prefer to hold include

_____

_____

_____

_____

_____

Some better beliefs around my health and well-being that I'd prefer to hold include:

_____

_____

_____

_____

_____

Some better beliefs around my appearance or weight that I'd prefer to hold include:

_____

_____

_____

_____

_____

Some better beliefs around other ideas I identified as having a detrimental impact on my life, that I'd prefer to hold include:

_____

_____

_____

_____

_____

Whilst part of you may not be totally on board with the new ideas and beliefs at first, and it may feel like you're making it up, don't worry. Just keep consciously choosing to hold onto the possibility that the new ideas will create better outcomes in your life, until you see the evidence of that happening. A few mantras, affirmations and visualisations will help you to embed the new beliefs, and enable you to re-programme yourself.

AFFIRMATIONS AND MANTRAS

An affirmation in this context is a statement of something that we wish to bring about in our lives, worded as though it was already true. For example, if you want to improve your health, "I am fit and well" is a great affirmation. "I want to stop feeling sick and tired all the time" is a pretty lousy one! Some of the best affirmations are stated in the Personal (i.e. they're about you, and worded "I am...", "I have...", "I can...", etc); the Positive (they're about what you want, not what you don't want); and the Present tense (they're stated as if it's true now, rather than something you want to happen in the future).

Every thought we think and statement we make produces associative images and feelings and inspires a particular kind of action. The statement "I am fit and well" is received at the deeper levels of mind and body and (when made in terms of the results we want to bring about), creates an imprint within the mind of ourselves in a good state of fitness and health. It also creates a positive emotional feeling which has a strengthening effect on the immune and other bodily systems. You can read more about this, if liked, in Dr Candace Pert's book: *The Molecules of Emotion*, Pocket Books, 1999.

The statement "I want to stop feeling sick and tired all the time" is likely to produce a mental image of our body in poor state of health and well-being, along with a negative emotional feeling and an accompanying weakening effect on the immune and other bodily systems.

Some examples of affirmations include:

- Today is going to be a really, really, really good day
- I can and I will
- Whatever happens, I'll handle it
- I always have more than enough time to do what's most important
- All my needs are met abundantly, now and always
- I am safe and I am loved
- All is well.

Of course, you can create an affirmation for whatever you wish to bring about. The possibilities are endless! You could also search 'affirmations' online for inspiration. I particularly love Louise Hay's many books and resources, but preferences are subjective, and you'll be drawn to the materials and resources that will be most helpful to you.

Muscle testing, as used in the practice of applied kinesiology, demonstrates the inherent power of positive and negative thoughts and affirmations on the body. When we think or state a positive thought or a true one, our muscles become strong and can easily resist any pressure that's put upon them. When we think or state a negative or untrue thought, our muscles become weak and unable to resist the push or pull pressures put on them. Dr Daphna Slonim has some excellent videos demonstrating energy muscle testing on YouTube.

On a not too dissimilar theme to affirmations, a mantra is a sacred word or group of words from Sanskrit which are repeated over and over, often as much for their sound and vibration as for their meaning. They can be chanted or sung silently or aloud, and those that use them believe that doing so introduces a beneficial vibrational frequency to the body that can be mood enhancing and healing.

Mantras can be used (amongst other purposes) to break repetitive patterns of thought, to transform a difficult or painful emotional state, or to bring us back to the present moment. They are common to Hinduism, Buddhism, Jainism and Sikhism, and are sometimes included as part of yoga and meditation practices. Some common mantras include:

- Om (said to vibrate at 432 Hertz, which stills the mind)
- Sat Nam
- So hum / hum sa
- Om Mani Padme Hum

A Hawaiian mantra that's received a lot of attention in recent times is Ho'oponopono – a forgiveness mantra, which may be translated into English and repeated as: "I love you; I'm sorry; Please forgive me; Thank you". This is said to be very powerful, especially when we really connect with the words and invoke the feelings of love, regret, forgiveness and gratitude.

VISUALISATION

Visualisation is the process of creating mental images or movie-clips in our minds or imaginations. We do this all the time (often without realising it) and not always for picturing the positive things that we'd like to have happen in our lives. Often, we picture the worst-case scenarios or worry-based fantasies about bad things happening, relating to our specific fears and doubts.

Conscious visualisation (where we choose the images we want to visualise) can be a very powerful tool, and is often used in goal setting and performance improvement - particularly in the sporting arena where it seems that most athletes these days have some kind of regular mental visualisation practice.

Visualisation is the first step of the manifesting process. In author Stephen Covey's classic book, *The 7 Habits of Highly Effective People* (Free Press, 1989), he states that all things are created twice: first comes the mental creation or visualisation, then comes the physical creation. All human creations start with a strong, clear thought.

When using visualisation, it helps to engage as many of the senses as possible in order to create a more powerful impression – seeing, hearing, feeling (and maybe even smelling and tasting) whatever it is you'd like to make happen, and making these impressions as vivid as possible. It's also helpful to make visualisation a regular practice, as Jim Carrey did every night on Mulholland Drive in Hollywood before making the big-time. In fact, it's worth noting that many successful people say that they have used visualisation to help them achieve their goals, including Oprah Winfrey, Sir Richard Branson, Arnold

Schwartzenegger, Will Smith, Jay Z, Michael Jordon, Wayne Rooney and Lady Gaga.

A great process for visualisation is as follows. It's best to set aside a regular time of day for this activity if you can, when it's quiet and you won't be disturbed. First thing in the morning is perfect, and you can get results in as little as seven minutes a day according to Rhonda Byrne in her book *The Power* (Atria Books, 2010):

- Take a deep breath and tell yourself you're going to dedicate the next seven minutes or so (minimum) visualising what you want to create in your life.
- Close your eyes and imagine a screen in front of you – maybe a large HDTV or a movie screen.
- Make yourself comfortable, then imagine the lights dimming and the screen coming to life.
- Bring your goals to mind one by one, see them playing out on the screen in front of you in bright, bold colours. Make the images bigger and bring the screen closer to you if it helps. What can you hear? Turn the volume up if it's not quite loud enough. Notice the impact you are having on others. See those around you supporting you and willing you to succeed. You are currently viewing these events from the outside looking in, so now, find a scene or two that you'd like to experience more deeply, and imagine that you've stepped into the screen and are inside your body, experiencing those scenes from behind your eyeballs. What can you see now? What can you hear? More importantly, what are you feeling? Feel how

amazing it's going to feel when you've achieved these goals. Breathe deeply and maximise those feelings now. What can you smell or taste, if anything? Stay with these feelings and impressions for a while, keeping them intense.

- Do this with each of your goals, and when you've finished, thank your mind for its co-operation and tell it that you know that this or something even better is already yours - just waiting for the perfect moment to materialise.

- Have faith that your goals can all come to fruition, and take an action every day that will take you closer towards them.

- Keep your focus, hold the vision and don't give up, unless for some reason those goals become unimportant to you, or something even better happens that takes their place.

Tools that can support visualisation include dream/vision boards (usually lots of different pictures cut out and stuck on a large piece of cardboard, reflecting your dreams and goals); mood boards (similar to dream/vision boards but reflecting how you want to feel); Pinterest collages; screen-savers; creation boxes (a shoebox or similar where you place pictures and items that represent what you want to bring into your life); guided visualisation apps and downloads. You can also draw or paint pictures to symbolise what you want – maybe dividing a large piece of paper up into 8 sections or boxes, representing goals for your Home, Work, Health/Well-being, Friends & Family, Leisure/Recreation, Love/Romance, Finances and Personal Development.

Using even one or two of these tools can be enough to help you design and create the results you want – just be sure to review your visuals often so they become firmly imprinted on your mind.

FEELINGISATION

Feelingisation is like visualisation but is centred around feeling. Visualising what we want on its own might not bring our goals to life without also creating a strong emotional impression. Creating a strong emotional impression is also likely to speed up the manifesting process, bringing what you want to you sooner than it might otherwise take. Here's the basic process:

- Take a deep breath and tell yourself you are now going to dedicate the next seven minutes or so (minimum) feeling what you want to create in your life.
- Close your eyes, and take three long, slow breaths in and out.
- Place your awareness within your heart. Imagine breathing into your heart, with it expanding and contracting along with your breath.
- Take a moment to feel love, gratitude and joy in your heart. Imagine breathing these feelings into your heart.
- Now, think about what you want and focus on the feelings you'll experience once you get those things. Really ramp up those feelings to create a strong, positive, emotional charge, and enjoy staying with them for a while.
- Do this for each of your goals, and when you've finished, thank your heart for its co-operation. Know that this or something even better will happen for you in due course.

- Take an action every day that will take you closer to your goals. Keep your focus and don't give up.

We can also use feelingisations in the mornings to set our emotional state for the day. For example, look ahead to your tasks and appointments for the day... what kind of feelings will support your success today? What will you need to feel strong and confident, energized, calm, focused, relaxed, playful, etc? Use the process just described to summon up these feelings – maybe remembering past times when you've felt those emotions, if it helps. Then, stubbornly refuse to allow anyone or anything that happens, to take you out of those feelings. Breathe, stay calm and remind yourself you always have a choice in what to feel, then stand firm in your intention to feel that way all day.

CHAPTER 3 SUMMARY

✓ We all carry some programming that's unhelpful, untrue or only partially true. However, this programming is just a collection of thoughts and ideas, and it's relatively straight-forward to drop the incorrect/unhelpful stuff once we become conscious of it, and swap it out for new, more helpful thoughts and ideas instead. If your programming was formed as a result of traumatic events, or if you're finding it hard to release old programming, you may wish to work with a therapist or coach for support.

✓ Affirmations are positive statements about what you wish to bring about, phrased as if they were already true. Repeating affirmations can help you to reprogramme yourself with more constructive, enabling thoughts, ideas and beliefs. The more often you repeat them, the more likely they are to stick. You might like to think of old vinyl records – smashing up the old ones that you don't want to listen to anymore and recording some new, better ones. Each time you repeat a new affirmation, the needle creates a deeper groove in the record, imprinting it more firmly.

✓ Mantras (repeated words and sounds) can be helpful in soothing the mind and introducing a more beneficial vibrational frequency to the body. They can form part of a daily prayer, meditation, yoga or similar practice, or just be used in the moment of need.

✓ Visualisation is the process of using our imagination to picture what we want to happen in our lives. It is one of the first steps in the manifestation process (more on this in Chapter 6).

✓ Feelingisation is the process of using our emotions to feel what we want to happen in our lives. If we don't create a strong emotional impression along with the thoughts of what we want, it's much less likely to manifest for us.

"IF YOU REALISED HOW POWERFUL YOUR THOUGHTS ARE, YOU'D NEVER THINK A NEGATIVE THOUGHT AGAIN"

- PEACE PILGRIM -
(MILDRED LISETTE NORMAN)

Chapter 4

OUR THINKING CAN BE OUR KRYPTONITE

We might not realise it (in fact, we may well deny it) but many of us do a fair amount of faulty, unhelpful and/or negative thinking. This can have the same debilitating effect on us as Kryptonite has on Superman – draining our energy and diminishing our power. It can also create problems and dysfunction in our lives.

Here are some facts about thinking:

- Most of us experience an almost constant stream of thought
- We can lack focus and experience our thinking as jumping about (the 'monkey mind')
- Sometimes we experience a lack of mental clarity (known as 'brain fog')
- We don't always thinking calmly, logically and rationally
- Many of us are fear-based (stemming from our in-built negativity bias)

- We can sometimes overthink things and create problems that aren't there
- We can confuse beliefs with facts
- Much of what we currently 'know' is faulty or limited in its truth
- We delete / distort / generalise, and make other thinking errors
- We are biased in some regards
- We can project past experiences into the present, creating 'Groundhog Day' scenarios
- We can get stuck in repetitive thinking loops
- Many of our thoughts today are the same as we had yesterday
- We tend to believe everything we think.

The term 'negative thinking' isn't necessarily about being cynical or pessimistic. It can incorporate a variety of different kinds of faulty and unhelpful thinking, which we will look at in this chapter.

Most of us develop at least some of this kind of thinking during our lives, and it can really get in the way of our health, happiness and success. It can include overthinking (many of us are compulsive thinkers, spending too much time up in our heads – often unproductively so); worry; fear; doubt; criticism; comparison; perfectionism (which may have a positive intent, but can have a negative impact); foggy and scattered thinking (where we lack clarity and/or jump about in our minds from one idea to another with no real flow or sequence); and plain old faulty and distorted thinking (incorrect 'knowledge', faulty/negative/limiting beliefs and concepts, poor attitudes, questionable values, unhelpful mindsets, and so on). Let's explore these one by one.

OVERTHINKING

Firstly, thinking is generally a helpful thing to do! It enables us to understand the world and successfully navigate the situations we find ourselves in. There's nothing wrong with thinking - in fact our thinking can be our superpower – energising and enabling us to resolve our problems and challenges, achieve our goals and live rewarding lives, but it can also be our Kryptonite, draining and disabling (even sabotaging) us, and keeping us from moving forwards in life.

Thinking too deeply, or for too long, can be a problem. Maybe we worry about all the different possibilities and outcomes (especially worst-case scenarios), or obsess about one situation or subject to the detriment of a balanced life. Perhaps we take a small scenario that happened - maybe something somebody said to us in a particular way - and turn it into a major incident in our minds, reading something into it that just wasn't there. Maybe we say something to someone in a particular way and then worry and obsess afterwards that they may have misunderstood somehow or taken it in the wrong way. Or, we may be guilty of 'analysis paralysis', going around in circles or getting tied up in knots in our minds, never quite reaching a conclusion or deciding on a course of action.

I love the story of McGinty's plow (below), which describes in a comical way how we can sometimes overthink things, and how our thinking can sometimes wander down a negative spiral. It helps to read it in a west-country accent!

Farmer McGinty needed to plough his field before the dry spell set in, but his plough had broken. "I know, I'll ask my neighbour, farmer Murphy, to borrow his plough. I'm sure he'll have done his ploughing by now and he'll be glad to lend it to me."

McGinty begins to walk the few fields towards Murphy's farm. After a while, he thinks to himself, "I hope Murphy has finished his ploughing or he'll not be able to lend me his machine..."

After a few more minutes of worrying and walking, he thinks to himself, "And what if his plough is old and on its last legs - he won't be wanting to lend it to me then..."

After another field, he's thinking, "Murphy was never a helpful fellow, I reckon he won't lend me his plough even if it's in perfect order and he finished his own ploughing weeks ago...."

As he gets to his neighbour's farm he thinks, "Murphy can be a mean old fellow. I reckon even if he's got all his ploughing done and his own machine is sitting doing nothing, he'll not lend it to me just to watch me go to ruin..."

He walks up the pathway, knocks on the door and Murphy answers, "Ah, good morning neighbour, what can I do for you today?" and McGinty replies, with eyes bulging, "You can take your bloody plough and you can shove it up your arse!".

Have your thoughts ever spiralled off in a similar fashion?!

Left to our own devices, many of us will think pretty much all the time. We don't give ourselves enough brain-breaks – moments where we detach from our thoughts and reconnect with our breathing or our senses. Overthinking can be exhausting, and the more thoughts we tend to have tumbling around 'up there', the less we can see the wood for the trees.

According to various online sources, an article published by the National Science Foundation in 2005, the average person has between 12,000 and 60,000 thoughts a day, of which 80% are said to be negative and 95% are said to be the same thoughts they had the day before.

It's not hard to see how overthinking could leave someone feeling tired and muddled! When we catch ourselves caught in loops and/or tied up in knots with our thinking, it helps to stop, breathe, and ask ourselves the following questions:

- Am I overthinking this?
- Is there something I can do about this situation? (If not, firmly tell your mind to drop the subject).

- Is now the best time to work through these thoughts, or am I getting ahead of myself? If not now, when?
- Would it be useful to talk this through with someone? (Often, when we externalise our thoughts and get them out of our heads, we see the situation for what it is with far greater clarity).
- Would it be useful to write a few things down? (See comment above).
- What's the situation, what's my concern, and what do I want?
- What are the facts, and am I sure they're true? Could my thinking be faulty in some way?
- What are my options? (Be wary of limiting yourself here). What else could I do?
- Thoughts aside, what does my heart (or intuition) tell me I should do?
- What would the consequences of these actions be, on all concerned?
- Do I feel good about this course of action? (If so, go for it! If not, consider other potential courses of action).
- You can adapt these questions to suit your situation.

WORRY

Worry is a form of overthinking, and describes repetitive thinking relating to actual or potential problems, resulting in a feeling of being anxious or troubled. When we worry, we are usually imagining negative outcomes. In a way, worry is a natural part of being human that's linked to our survival. It can lead us to resourceful thinking in terms of risk management and contingency planning, and in this way, it serves us in moderation. However, we can sometimes get stuck in negative imaginings, and fail to move into the kind of constructive, solution-focused thinking that enables us to address our problems. Worry is just a misuse of the imagination. Without resourceful action, it robs us of today's joy and peace, whilst doing nothing to take away tomorrow's troubles.

Worries and concerns typically go around and around inside our heads in an unproductive way, without us reaching any kind of clarity or resolution on them until we externalise them. Once they've been externalised, we can see them for what they are – just problems and challenges that there's probably a way forward with, or a solution to, if we researched our options or asked someone for help.

A colleague of mine uses the analogy of a tumble dryer to describe the mind. If we look at the contents inside, we'll find that there's all sorts of stuff going around in there daily, but a worry or concern is a bit like a red sock. It grabs our attention, and all we can really focus on is the sock. When we open the door and remove the contents (i.e. externalise the thoughts by talking about them or writing them down), we're able to see everything in front of us from a more detached, observer's position. It also helps us get a sense of proportion and perspective on the problem or concern... that there are plenty of things on going in our lives - many of them pretty good or at least manageable. The red sock is just one part that, now we can see it for what it is, doesn't seem quite so overwhelming.

When we talk to others about our red sock, we might find that they've experienced something similar too (or know someone who has), and that we're not on our own, and there are actions we can explore that could help us move forward.

At the risk of making generalisations, women more readily share their thoughts and feelings with others, and also, tend to be more strongly socially networked than men. Historically, in many cultures, we've brought our boys up with messages about being brave, keeping a 'stiff upper lip', growing a pair, etc., that suggest showing emotion is a sign of weakness, and that boys shouldn't cry. The result has been generations of men who have bottled up their emotions all through their lives (sometimes numbing them with alcohol and other substances), and who haven't felt able to express them for fear of being perceived as weak, aggressive, or as failures.

At the time of writing, the UK and the US share similar statistics on male suicide, with around three quarters of all suicide deaths being male – a situation that a number of organisations and agencies are currently seeking to improve.

Things are changing, thankfully, and schools in some countries are teaching children the skills of emotional literacy and emotional intelligence. Younger men and women seem to be much more able to aptly voice their needs, expectations, problems and concerns, and this can only be a good thing.

One thing we can probably all do is encourage and reassure each other – and perhaps particularly our men – that it's ok to be emotionally honest, to ask for help when we're struggling and to empty our tumble dryers when we have a worry or concern churning around in there.

Sometimes we don't want to 'burden' our friends and family with our problems, or even to feel judged by them, and in these situations, counselling and coaching can be very helpful. Charities like Samaritans in the UK and Ireland exist in many countries, where you can access free emotional support through a telephone helpline, and in some cases, online via email and text. Samaritans' helpline in the UK is open 24/7/365 and is not just for people who are feeling suicidal. Seventy-eight percent of those using the service just want to talk to someone who will listen to them without judgement or telling them what to do. From the UK, we can dial 116 123. More information can be found at www.samaritans.org.

Anyone that doesn't want to talk to someone else about a worry they have could opt to follow these simple steps instead:

1. Write down the situation that's causing concern and what specifically is worrying you about it.
2. Ask yourself if your concern is rational – for example, is the thing you're worrying about genuinely likely to happen and if it did, what would the real impact be?
   - If it's not very likely and/or the impact wouldn't be that bad, you could choose to do nothing but breathe deeply, tell yourself to relax and visualise the worry as a red, helium-filled balloon that you release at the top of a hill and watch drift away.
   - If it is quite likely and/or it would have a significant impact if it happened, complete the remaining steps
3. Do some research and identify all the possible courses of action open to you. Decide which of these would be the most effective.
4. Take the relevant action, getting help if needed. Trust that whatever happens, you'll handle it and that everything is always working out for you.
5. If the worry thoughts continue, take yourself to a quiet place, relax and imagine the conscious, rational part of your mind talking to your subconscious mind, telling it that everything is under control and it can just relax and trust that all will be well. Don't underestimate the power of visualisation in these matters.

6. If you have religious or spiritual beliefs, surrender the situation to the higher power, asking for assistance and holding the vision of the best possible outcome. Take any further action that you feel inspired to take.

For anyone whose worries have turned to thoughts of suicide, Feelgood Farm in Anstey, near Leicester, is a community wellness centre that combines a suicide sanctuary with a café, wellbeing therapies, music, arts and more. Owned and run by founder of www.BusinessBalls.com website Alan Chapman, you can find out more at www.feelgoodfarm.co.uk, or email enquiries to ac@alanchapman.com. Other sanctuaries exist in the UK and elsewhere, and the internet is a good source of information.

FEAR

Fear is prevalent, and is believed to be one of the strongest motivating factors in human behaviour. Only two fears are said to be innate within in all people – the fear of falling and the fear of loud noises - both of which we are said to be born with. Some fears are thought to be genetically inherited from our parents or ancestors, for example, the fear of snakes, rats, and so on; other fears are simply learnt through experience, like the fear of dogs (having been bitten in childhood), or of people you don't know (perhaps as a result of over-zealous safety warnings in childhood).

As author and activist Marianne Williamson says, "Love is what we were born with. Fear is what we learned here". In fact, love is the very best antidote to fear that exists.

Clearly, some fears are sensible and keep us safe from harm. All fears seek to protect us from bad things happening and can be useful to a point. Often though, our fears can be somewhat limiting, for example the fear of judgement, failure, rejection, commitment, loss, humiliation, poverty, social situations, and so on. These fears can stop us from relaxing, fulfilling our potential and living a full and wonderful life. Some can cause high levels of anxiety and stress.

Many of our fears are irrational (as in the acronym FEAR – False Evidence Appearing Real), fear being nothing more than fabricated illusions of the mind. Our fears are just thoughts that we think, and they aren't even real, but this doesn't stop them from feeling real. In fact, the fear of something happening can often feel worse than if the thing actually happened!

To follow is a list of common fears. Place a tick next to any that apply to you, then give them a score out of 10 for severity (10 being highest), noting how the fear is influencing your life:

Fear	✓	0-10	How the fear is limiting or influencing your life
Abandonment/being alone			
Change/the unknown			
Commitment			
Death/ill health			

Fear	✓	0-10	How the fear is limiting or influencing your life
Failure			
Humiliation			
Inadequacy			
Intimacy			
Judgement/disapproval			
Loss			
Pain (inc. emotional)			
Poverty			
Rejection			
Social situations			
Success			

We will probably all experience some of these events in our lives and come through them. The thought is often worse than the reality. Recognise that your fears are largely illusions, but that, even if they did happen, it probably wouldn't be the end of the world (except in the case of death, although it could be argued even that isn't the end, but rather, just the start of a new adventure!).

Sometimes our fears are so strong and anxiety provoking that they become phobias (commonly, speaking in public, flying, heights, spiders, snakes, death, germs, needles, dentists, hospitals, open/enclosed spaces, and so on).

There's a saying that everything we want is on the other side of fear. Most of us think of fear as meaning 'Stop!' but what if it really means 'Go ahead!' – at least in the situations where our lives aren't at risk? Facing our fears is usually confidence building, and results in them losing their power.

Take a few moments to write down any fears or phobias you have and wish to overcome, and what you could do to address these. Think about all the different kinds of resources that might help you. There are loads of books, online learning programmes, training workshops, support groups, therapists and coaches dedicated to helping you overcome your specific fear or problem. Why not go online now and do a bit of research – find out what help is out there? Make some notes in the table below:

Fear or Phobia	Actions I will take to help myself overcome it

Fear or Phobia	Actions I will take to help myself overcome it

DOUBT

Doubt is a feeling of uncertainty that lies somewhere between can and can't, belief and disbelief, safe and unsafe (etc). Look up the opposite of doubt and you will find words like certainty, conviction, confidence, faith and belief.

Aside from death, taxes and near-constant change, not many things in life are certain! Also, most if not all of us experience self-doubt and a lack of confidence in some area of our lives. We are naturally better at some things than others, and whilst we can probably learn to do anything we put our minds to, we won't be brilliant at absolutely everything.

Sometimes it's not our ability that we doubt, but our looks, personality or character. Maybe on some level we doubt that we're really good enough, and live our lives hoping that we don't get found out, as is the case for those suffering from Imposter Syndrome (defined as: "The persistent inability to believe that one's success is deserved, or has been legitimately achieved as a result of one's own efforts or skills"). Reportedly, 70% of people experience Imposter Syndrome at some time during their lives, including talented and successful people like David Bowie, Lady Gaga, Maya Angelou, Serena Williams, Natalie Portman, Tom Hanks and Emma Willis, to name just a few. If you've ever experienced these kinds of thoughts, I hope you will find this reassuring. You are in excellent company! It's not just you – it seems to be most people, to some extent at least.

The truth is that everyone's good at something, and no-one's good at everything. There's a reason for this. We all have a place and purpose in life, and we are always good enough when we play to our strengths, do what we love, and do our best. Will we fail at some things? Probably, yes - although what we call 'failure' could actually be seen as success in progress (like in the acronym FAIL - First Attempt In Learning)!

In working out what we love and are good at, we may well stumble across some things that we're not so good at, and this is par for the course. These experiences help guide us towards a path and purpose that plays to our strengths and that feels good to us.

Maybe it's not self-doubt that's a thing for us as much as it's doubting other people. Perhaps it's doubting the things that we haven't seen with our own eyes, or doubting our safety and security. Doubt is reasonable and rational in many ways (for example, we shouldn't take everything we hear or read on face value), and blind faith can seem naïve and childlike. However, doubt can be overblown.

When we doubt others, it can cause them to doubt themselves, which is very disempowering and can take away their confidence – even reducing their ability. Have you ever worked for a manager who believed in you, gave you stretch tasks and projects, and you thrived and did great things? Have you ever worked for a manager who doubted you, gave you no development, and your performance floundered? Doubt has a powerfully negative impact.

Building on the theme of uncertainty that's a characteristic of doubt, we are living in very interesting times. The acronym VUCA (standing for Volatile, Uncertain, Complex and Ambiguous) originated in the US Army in the late 1980s, and was used to describe the period during and after the Cold War. The term has since been adopted more widely to describe the world that we find ourselves in today – essentially one where the pace of change is unprecedented, where few things are predictable, where we are enmeshed in complex interdependencies, and where the future is rather unclear.

To survive and thrive in such a world requires something of a leap of faith. On the face of things, we're living in perilous times, with war, terrorism, global warming, over-population, disease, and so on, all being potential threats; and yet many of us have an inner sense that, whatever happens, it's going to be ok – that fundamentally we are safe and all is well. This may be the case for those that believe that our essence is spiritual, and can't really be destroyed – even if our physical bodies are. It's interesting that in a crisis, even the non-religious can find themselves praying or asking unseen forces for help. Perhaps a part of us recognises the spiritual nature of existence, even if our rational, thinking minds don't!

If we catch ourselves doubting our safety in the world, it's worth cultivating the sense (or inner knowing?) that all is well, and that we are safe. Whatever happens, it probably won't mean the end of the world, and even if it is the end of the world and our physical bodies perish, the part of us that is eternal and invincible will live on.

Whilst I don't believe there's absolute, concrete evidence for this currently, and it can therefore only be classified as a belief, it's one that enables me to relax and feel better about life. I'm not a religious person as such, but I do have a sense of an all-loving, all-providing power in the universe that supports us. As beliefs tend to be self-fulfilling, regardless of whether they are true or not, I figure that just holding these thoughts will probably keep me safer than if I was to walk around with a head full of thoughts of impending doom! I hope they will bring a sense of comfort and security to you too.

We might not be able to do much personally in terms of changing what's happening in the wider world, but we can consider what we could do in our small corner of it to make it as great as we can. This could start with surrendering our fear-based illusions, and trusting that whatever happens, things generally turn out ok in the end.

Trusting ourselves, trusting others and trusting the process of life might seem radical, but, as is the case with love, trust is an excellent antidote to worry, fear and doubt. Worrying about things we can't change is a waste of energy and doesn't improve the situation. It serves us so much better to simply focus on what's here, now and real.

CRITICISM

Criticism is about judgement - usually fault-finding and disapproval, although it can be offered with a positive intent, as is the case in constructive criticism. That said, it has a negative feel to it, and might not lead to positive action.

On the receiving end, criticism can be helpful if we allow ourselves to grow from it rather than be diminished. We don't have to feel hurt by it if we refuse to let that happen. Instead, we can look for the bit that could prove useful to us whilst rejecting any bits that are untrue, hurtful or destructive. We shouldn't automatically reject criticism, though, without taking some time to non-defensively consider its validity.

On the giving end, criticism can often be met with defensiveness, and yet, many people are open to feedback that they know will be helpful to them, and this tends to have a different feel to it.

Criticism directed towards ourselves isn't helpful, but honest self-appraisal can be. Aim to give yourself feedback in a way that you'd offer it to a dear friend or beloved child. Make sure it's balanced, and that you see it in perspective of the many good features you also have.

Do this when giving others feedback too. We may notice the negatives in others more readily than their strengths. If we want good relationships, we should try to look out for, and appreciate, the positives in others. People often feel our judgements of them, and that's what they tend to reflect back to us. Appreciate them and they will give you more things to appreciate. Criticise them and they will give you more things to criticise.

Essentially, be a lover, not a hater! Being loving feels good to us – we benefit as much as the recipient. The world needs a bit more love and kindness right now. The famous IKEA experiments (admittedly non-scientific) demonstrated that flowers and plants flourished when they were spoken to with love (i.e. when they received positive sound vibrations) and withered when they were spoken to with hatred (when they received negative sound vibrations). Interestingly, a similar but separate experiment carried out by the Royal Horticultural Society showed that plants spoken to by a female voice grew more quickly than those spoken to by a male voice, although the researchers couldn't say for sure why this was.

COMPARISON

Comparison, on the face of things, probably doesn't appear to be the greatest of thinking crimes. However, its effects can be quite heinous.

No matter who we are and what aspect of ourselves we are measuring, there will always be others who are better and worse than we are. Our egos tend to get a little boost when we find that we're better than someone else in some way, and they can crumble when we find that we aren't as good, but none of it really matters. The fact is that we will be better, stronger, nicer looking (and so on) than some people, and not as good as others. It's just the way things are.

Our sense of value and being an OK and worthwhile person shouldn't be tied up with our ability, appearance or anything else other than who we are on the inside, at our essence.

Often, we are compared as children with our siblings and peers, and this can create feelings of inadequacy. We are who we are, and should compare ourselves (and our children) with no-one.

Social media has a lot to answer for, as we see the doctored photos and glossy highlights of other people's lives, and could feel like we need to try and compete with them, or maybe feel like we are failing in comparison.

Do the best you can and stop comparing yourself to others, or you will never be happy. The only basis for true happiness and connection is recognising that you were born equal to all others – that no man or woman is greater or lesser than another. Go and read the Universal Declaration of Human Rights if you are in any doubt.

PERFECTIONISM

The dictionary defines 'perfect' as being without fault or defect. Perfectionism is a trait where a person sets impossibly high standards of perfection for themselves and/or others, with the result that they feel consistently disappointed and even stressed, because life and human beings rarely (if ever) live up to the definition of 'perfect'. For this reason, perfectionism is linked to low self-esteem.

Perfectionism is different to striving for excellence, in that it leaves no room for error, and is more obsessive in its nature. Striving for excellence can be a good thing, but obsessively trying to attain perfection is futile because (according to Plato's Theory of Forms) it doesn't exist in the physical world.

If you're a perfectionist, you will never quite feel good enough, and other people will usually fall short of your standards and expectations too. Make it a goal to give up your perfectionism and focus on always doing the best you can instead. Be gentle with yourself and others, knowing that you and they will sometimes makes mistakes, and won't always be good at everything.

'Be Perfect' is one of five unconscious drivers of behaviour identified by Taibi Kahler in the 1970s. The other four are 'Be Strong', 'Hurry Up', 'Please Others' and 'Try Hard'. These statements (or words like them) are often repeated to us in childhood, and act like instructions embedded into the deeper part of our minds, that we can still be unconsciously following into our adulthood.

Within reason these can serve us well, but when they become overblown, they can drive unhelpful behaviours and cause us problems. For example, if we feel that we always must always be perfect, be strong, hurry up, please others and try hard, that's not healthy.

Do any of these behaviour drivers resonate with you? If so, which ones? What effects have they been having on your life? For example, where have they been useful to you and where have they not been helping? Make some notes:

_____

_____

_____

_____

_____

_____

_____

_____

_____

_____

_____

_____

_____

_____

What if you could drop them or replace them with something more realistic and helpful? How might that change the results you're getting in life and in work?

Just telling yourself, "I do not always have to be perfect / be strong / hurry up / please others / try hard" can take the pressure off, and make you feel less stressed.

FOGGY AND SCATTERED THINKING

Some people experience a lack of clarity in their thinking – often referred to as brain fog. Others find it difficult to focus, concentrate, or remember names, words, appointments, and so on. These symptoms can be constant or intermittent, and can be caused by many different factors including (but not limited to):

- Stress
- Too many 'open tabs' (i.e. too many lines of thought open at the same time – multitasking)
- Conditions like chronic fatigue, MS, fibromyalgia, Hashimoto's/thyroid deficiency
- Chemo brain (cognitive impairment following chemotherapy)
- Hormone changes (pregnancy brain, menopause brain)
- Poor diet (too much sugar, refined carbohydrates, bad fats; too little protein, fresh fruit and vegetables)
- Food allergies and intolerances, especially gluten (found in many grains) and dairy foods, but also peanuts, MSG, artificial sweeteners and others
- Lack of sleep (less than 7 hours, and you will probably notice some cognitive impairment)
- Dehydration (around 2 litres/8 glasses of water a day is needed for the average person)
- Sedentary lifestyle (getting your circulation going through exercise – even brisk walking – will provide your brain with the oxygen and nutrients it needs).

Sometimes our thinking is not so much foggy, as scattered. Buddhist teachings describe the human mind as being like a drunken monkey – swinging haphazardly from branch to branch (or idea to idea), unsettled, easily distracted and sometimes confused.

Our brains are designed to constantly seek new information, so I suspect this rapid thought association was intended as a design feature to aid our survival. In some ways it serves us well, although that's clearly not the case when we need to focus, concentrate and see a task through to completion. It's therefore useful to learn how to calm our monkey-minds down when needed, and direct them in more focused and sequential ways. We can do this by engaging in the following activities:

- Stopping multitasking – dealing with one thing (or groups of similar tasks) at a time
- Taking notifications off our phones
- Keeping our phones on silent when we need to, or leaving them in another room
- Having set times when we go online or check our email accounts, and sticking to them
- Keeping a clear and tidy environment
- Learning to meditate
- Practising mindfulness
- Building regular bouts of physical activity into our schedule
- Drinking more water
- Taking short breaks every 90 minutes or so
- Doodling when we need to focus or listen for long periods of time (especially when taking pictorial notes)
- Eating fresh, whole foods (oily fish is especially good), and avoiding refined carbs, sugar and salt.

Mindfulness can be helpful for those with scattered thinking. For something that was once pretty much the territory of only

Buddhist Monks, mindfulness has become something of a movement in the West in recent years, having been adopted by celebrities, the corporate world and regular people alike.

The 'always on' culture of communication technology can create feelings of stress and overwhelm, and be a barrier to relaxation. Many of us are juggling multiple responsibilities at work and at home, meaning that mind-fulness (where our minds are so full most of the time that we are not able to be mentally present to the moment we are in) has become the norm. This is exhausting and unsustainable, and probably explains the current popularity of mindfulness and other forms of meditation, which enable us to relax our minds and reconnect to the present moment.

John Kabat-Zinn was one of the biggest influencers in bringing mindfulness to the West. He describes mindfulness as, "Paying attention in a particular way: on purpose, in the present moment and non-judgementally." This can mean paying attention to the external world – the sights, sounds, sensations, smells and tastes, and to our internal world – becoming conscious of our thoughts and emotions.

Mindfulness can be a regular practice – maybe 5 or 10 minutes at the start and end of every day, or it can be practiced randomly during waking hours, when engaging in activities like walking, eating, doing the washing up, and so on. It can be focused around just one of the senses, or on several.

In mindfulness, focusing on the inner world can involve noticing thoughts, sensations and emotions. You don't have to try and change them as such – just bringing your awareness to them (and noticing their temporary nature) might be enough.

Mindfulness is just one form of meditation. There are many others, including the following simple ones which are good for beginners:

- **Breath awareness**. Sit comfortably and pay attention to the sensations of your breathing as it rises and falls. Don't try and change your breathing in any way – just follow its natural pattern.

- **Candle meditation**. Sit comfortably in a darkened room. Light a candle and place it on a solid surface near you (but not too close), at or slightly below eye-level, and taking care to ensure it's safe. Now, stare softly at the flame and imagine drawing light from the candle into and out of yourself as you breathe.

- **Progressive relaxation**. Lie down and, starting from your toes and working up to the top of your head, gradually place your awareness in each part of your body, telling each part to relax and let go of tension. Some people like to tense the muscles first then relax them. You can imagine sending healing light into each body part too if you like.

- **Loving kindness**. There are different versions of this - to follow is a simple one. Sit quietly and repeat these words, taking your time and allowing yourself to feel the emotion in the words as you speak them, before moving on to the next sentence: "May I be loving, and may I be loved; May I be kind, and may I attract kindness; May I show compassion, and may I receive compassion". Repeat this twice again (saying it three times in total). If there's a particular person with whom your relationship is strained or difficult, you could follow this version: "I send love to (person's name) – and I accept it back; I offer kindness to (person's name) – and I accept it back; I show compassion to (person's name) and I accept it back." Repeat this twice again (three times in total).

- **Guided meditation.** There are many free guided meditations available online, and many excellent subscription services too. Find one with a voice that sounds good to you, and sit or lie back and relax whilst the recording talks you through some guided imagery designed to relax you, heal you, reduce anxiety or do whatever you selected it for. You can find guided meditations that I've written and recorded on my website, at www.sunshinedevelopment.co.uk.

POOR MEMORY

Some of the tips and strategies covered in the section above on foggy and scattered thinking can also help improve memory, along with cutting back on alcohol, using brain-training games and taking certain nutritional supplements (ginkgo biloba, vitamin B12 and vitamin E being commonly recommended).

There is also a correlation between vitamin D deficiency and poor memory/cognitive decline, and whilst this isn't necessarily a causation, it's wise to get a daily dose of sunlight and fresh air. In fact, oxygenating your system is beneficial for every part of your body – not just your brain – so get your exercise outdoors if you can, and fill your lungs, knowing that in doing so you're more likely to stay healthy and disease free.

Revisiting memories in your mind, and refreshing yourself on past learning, are very good ways of ensuring you retain information. Personally, I need to review something 3 or 4 times before it really sticks. Continuous learning all through life is a great way of keeping your mind and memory functioning effectively, so it's good to try and learn something new - however small - every day if you can, and maybe also learn a new skill at least every year.

Check out learning and memory maestro Tony Buzan's body of work for more tips and strategies: www.tonybuzan.com.

FAULTY THINKING

Faulty thinking is a big subject area, and there are many ways in which our thinking can be faulty. To start with, we all carry around a bunch of knowledge and 'facts' that are probably far from true. For example, according to myth-busting information available online, Napoleon wasn't short for his time, at around 5ft 7ins; spinach isn't especially high in iron, sugar doesn't make children hyper-active (maybe it's the E-number additives often attached to sugar that do that); carrots don't help you see in the dark; bats aren't blind – their eyesight is reasonably good; Buddha wasn't fat and bald (the big guy often assumed to be Buddha was a Chinese Buddhist monk); Thomas Edison didn't invent the light bulb; Thomas Crapper didn't invent the flushing toilet; teeth aren't supposed to be white; mice aren't overly fond of cheese; goldfish have very good memories; and many scientific studies are ultimately proved wrong.

It's very hard to know exactly what is and isn't true unless you can personally trace it back to its original source and verify the data, which is unlikely in many cases. Suffice to say that it's best to keep an open mind about everything you've ever read, been told or assumed to be true, because it's likely that a significant proportion of this is faulty or flawed in some way.

We're all brought up with certain values, attitudes, beliefs and concepts relating to ourselves, other people, life and everything, and we tend to accept these as 'true' – after all, they're usually given to us by our parents or other authority figures that we trust and don't question (as young children, at least). Depending on the individuals that raise us; the friends we have; the schools we go to; the country we live in; the decade we're born in; whether we're male, female or other; and a multitude of other factors, many of our beliefs and concepts will differ to what others believe. Who's to say who's right or wrong - or indeed, if there even is a universal right and wrong, in some cases. It doesn't serve us to hold onto ideas too tightly or to accept everything that we read or are told, unquestioningly. Our intuition can help us to recognise truth when we see or hear it, so we just need to do our research, use our discernment and trust our inner guidance.

A multitude of different thinking errors and cognitive biases have been identified and classified over the years, highlighting how we delete, distort and generalise the information that comes to us. The following model illustrates:

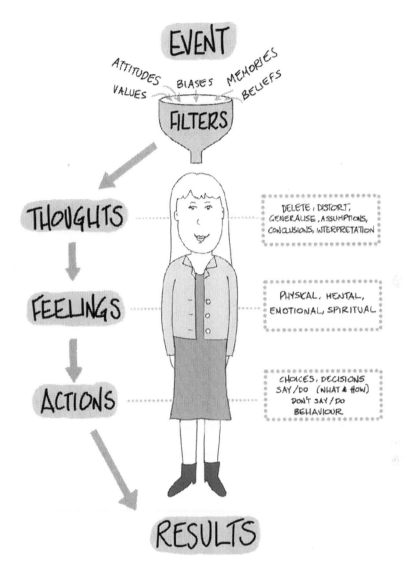

In simple terms, information comes to us via our senses - what we see, hear, touch, smell and taste. We then filter this information through our memories, biases, values, beliefs, attitudes, and so on, deciding which bits to ignore and which bits to pay attention to. We then form an interpretation or conclusion about it, and this generates an emotional and physical reaction that drives our actions and behaviour.

So, our perceptions aren't always based on how things really are but on information that we've deleted, distorted and generalised, based on our experience! This is what author Anais Nin meant when she said, "We don't see things as they are, we see them as we are."

To follow is a selection of some of the most common thinking errors that we're prone to making. As you read the descriptions that follow, think about times when you may have made those errors, and how you might safeguard against making them in the future:

FILTERING

Filtering is the term used to describe how we pay attention to certain negative details, whilst filtering out other positive ones. An example of this is noticing someone's negative qualities, and failing to see their good ones. Another is saying that we've had a terrible day, when one bad thing happened amongst 20 good things.

Most white van drivers and BMW owners on the road are courteous, but if we have a reference in our brain that suggests otherwise, we might only notice those that aren't.

Can you think of any situations where you're guilty of filtering out positive information? What might the consequences of this be?

The next time you catch yourself noticing negative details and making judgements, ask yourself these questions: "Might I be selectively filtering here? Am I failing to notice (this person's good or bad points / the courteous drivers all around me?). Am I believing a story or myth that I've heard? What else might I notice or observe if I opened my mind?"

PERSONALISATION

Personalisation is when we assume that something negative that happens is about us personally - seeing ourselves as the cause, and taking the blame when it wasn't our fault.

One example of this is when someone is snappy or rude to us and we take it personally, wondering what we've done to upset them rather than concluding that they're perhaps a bit stressed or generally unhappy.

Another example is when a child experiences a failure, and the parent believes it's a failure on *their* part - that perhaps they didn't help the child enough, instead of concluding that the failure is all part of the learning process, and that there's a bit more learning for their child to do before success can be theirs.

When was the last time you took something personally when it might have been nothing to do with you at all?

To overcome personalisation, understand that other people's behaviour is generally more about them than it is about you. When you find yourself taking things personally, ask yourself, "What assumptions am I making, and is this really about me? What else could this be about?". It is also helpful to focus on strengthening your self-esteem, so you don't automatically assume that you are the cause of everything negative.

POLARISED THINKING

Polarised thinking is the term given to believing that things are either black or white, good or bad, right or wrong, or taking an 'all-or-nothing' approach to life. When our thinking is polarised in this way, we fail to notice the grey areas, variations, or full spectrum of possibilities. Part of us would probably prefer things to be simple and straight-forward, rather than nuanced and complex, as they often are. We see what we want to see.

One example of polarised thinking is avoiding the sun completely because you've heard it's bad for you. Another example is believing that if someone isn't a friend of yours, they must therefore be an enemy.

What examples of polarised thinking do you have from your own life? Are there some people or things that you've categorically defined as all-good or all-bad?

Ask yourself, "Is it really a case of (black or white / good or bad / right or wrong), or are there more dimensions than I'm noticing?"; "Is it always that way, or are things sometimes situational?"; "Do people really either love or hate Marmite, or could some people be a bit indifferent?!"

OVER-GENERALISING

Over-generalising is when we jump to an overly general conclusion about something, based on limited experience. This can have the effect of limiting our lives and making them less rich and varied.

Maybe you have your heart broken twice in your teenage years.

You make a generalisation that men/women can't be trusted, and vow never to give your heart to anyone again. Or perhaps, you go for a few interviews for promotion but don't get the jobs. You decide that you'll never become a manager because you're just not made of the right stuff.

What over-generalisations have you formed in life? They're the kind of statements that include the words always..., never..., everyone..., all..., etc. How might you be losing out because of these over-generalisations?

When you become conscious of your generalisations and sweeping statements ("Young people today..."; "Men/women always..."; "Things never go right..."), ask yourself, "Is it really all (young people/men/women/things) or just some?"; "How many aren't like that?"; "Which things have gone wrong recently, and which have gone well?"

CATASTROPHISING

Catastrophising is a form of negative, irrational thinking where we believe situations are far worse than they are.

For example, we may fail an exam and believe that our life is over... we will never amount to anything and will end up living under a bridge sleeping on cardboard. Or maybe, when we look into the future, we worry about everything that could go wrong: "What if [this] happens and I end up looking a fool? What if [that] happens and I have a terrible accident and can never walk again?"

These examples are a little extreme, but what are the ways in which you have imagined situations to be far worse than they really are? Maybe there's something happening right now that feels like the end of the world, but that heralds a wonderful new beginning that, in retrospect, you'll be thankful for.

When you become aware that your thoughts are running away with you, ask yourself, "Am I seeing things in perspective here? How likely is that to happen, and if did, would it really be as bad as I'm imagining?" Allow the sensible, rational part of yourself to calm the concerns of the part that tends to imagine the worst.

EMOTIONAL REASONING

This is when we feel a certain way about something, and assume that we must be right ("I feel... therefore it is...").

For example, thinking: "I really don't like that person, therefore there must be something wrong with them," or "I feel worthless, therefore I probably am worthless," or "I really think my partner's cheating on me. The feelings are so strong that I must be right".

Our emotions can be an excellent guide in life, helping to inform our decisions, and it can be foolish to ignore a strong, intuitive feeling. However, it's wise to employ both head and heart when making decisions, as our emotions can be influenced by our history and our fears, rather than by any real danger or risk.

What things do you believe that are purely based on how you feel? Can you be sure that how you feel truly reflects how things are?

Before taking any action that's driven by emotion, ask yourself, "Am I sure about this? Could my 'logic' be faulty?", "What facts haven't I considered?", "Are events from my past (that have no connection with this situation today) influencing my emotions?"

LABELLING

Labelling is where we take one characteristic of a person, place or thing, and apply it to the whole. Labels can be positive (clever, pretty, etc) or negative (stupid, lazy, etc), but whether they're positive or negative, they can limit us and others, as we might not see beyond those labels to everything else that the person, place or thing is.

An example of a negative label is when someone makes a silly mistake in the first few weeks of us knowing them. We label them an idiot, and consider them as such for the rest of time, failing to recognise their other great qualities and attributes.

Another example is driving through the back streets of a city on our way to somewhere else, and labelling it a dump. It will forever be a dump in our mind, despite its many amazing buildings and beauty spots, which we didn't see, and remain ignorant of.

What are the labels that you've attached to people, places and things (maybe even to yourself)? Remember that 'what you see is what you get' (acronym: 'Wysiwyg'!). When we open our minds to seeing things in a better/broader light, it improves our experience.

When you catch yourself applying labels, remember that this is just your subjective opinion based on limited information. Ask yourself (or others), "What are the other aspects of (the person / place / thing) that I might be missing out on?".

Finally, don't just accept the labels that you've been given. You are much more than someone's limited perception or description of you. Surprise yourself and others!

ALWAYS BEING RIGHT

This is where we believe that our beliefs and opinions are always the right ones. It's unthinkable that we might ever be wrong.

An example is having a disagreement with someone about something and going to ridiculous lengths to search for information that proves them wrong. If it transpires that we were wrong, the feeling is so unbearable that we'd do anything to avoid it and save face - even continuing to uphold our faulty position in the face of evidence to the contrary.

On what matters do you tend to think your opinion is the right one, or that you know best? Sometimes that might be the case, but you won't be right all the time because no-one is (including the 'experts').

Being wrong occasionally doesn't diminish you or make you lesser in any sense - it just makes you human. Practise saying things like: "I'm sorry - I can see now that I was wrong" until it feels OK.

There's a little bit of magic in admitting when we're wrong, and interestingly, doing so tends to make us rise in people's estimations rather than fall.

MIND-READING

This is when we think we know what other people are thinking without checking it out with them.

For example, imagine that someone is studying your face intently. You might think they must be finding faults with your appearance (or maybe you assume they're thinking how good looking you are!). Another example would be when you say something in a meeting and can almost 'hear' the person that doesn't seem to like you thinking: "What a load of rubbish!"

What examples do you have of times when you've read people's minds (i.e. assumed that you knew what they were thinking)?

We are often guilty of (mis)reading faces and making assumptions about what they mean, but some people just have unfortunate features or facial expressions (as in R.B.F, or resting bitch face!) and sometimes it just our paranoia.

Next time you make an assumption about what someone's thinking, realise that you might be wrong, and consider what else they might be thinking instead. Try asking a simple question to test your theory, for instance: "Mark, I might be wrong, but you look like you don't agree with my point. Am I right?"

We never really know for sure until we ask.

CONTROL FALLACIES

Control fallacies are where we assume we have an inaccurate amount of control, maybe believing we can control everything, or believing we can control nothing.

For example, we may think we can make someone change their behaviour, when the truth is that we can only ever hope to influence them; or we might feel unable to help ourselves out of a bad situation, believing that life is something that happens to us, and we have to just roll with it.

In truth, some things happen to us outside of our control - they have an external origin and we can't do anything about them; there are some things that we have some influence over, but only limited control; and there are other things that we have total control over (even if it doesn't always feel like it), such as our choices, decisions, actions and behaviours. We can only have full control over ourselves, and attempts to control external events and people can be very frustrating when they don't go as we'd like.

What are the kinds of things you try to control, or perhaps feel powerless over and don't even bother trying to influence?

If you're trying to control something external, and feeling frustrated or hopeless because you perceive you can't influence the situation or change your behaviour, check out your locus of control (the degree to which you believe you can control the outcome of events in your life). Ask yourself; "Am I trying to control something that in truth is outside of my control?", "Am I assuming there's nothing I can do to influence this?", or "Am I forgetting that I have a choice here (or pretending that I don't have one), and could choose to do something different in order to get a better result?"

In truth, we can influence most things with the right approach and support.

BLAMING

This is when we hold other people responsible for our feelings, actions and/or results.

For example, we might blame our manager for always making us feel bad about ourselves; we might lose patience with our children, yelling: "Don't make me shout at you!"; or maybe we blame our partner for making us fat, by feeding us too well!

Who do you blame, and for what?

Whilst other people can provide us with a strong invitation to feel or do something, we are all ultimately responsible for our own feelings, actions and outcomes. In truth, no-one else can make us feel or do anything - only our own thinking can do that. This means that we need to give up all blame and excuses, and ask ourselves: "What thoughts am I thinking that are making me feel or act this way? What can I take responsibility for, and what can I do to improve things?"

Whilst it's sometimes tough to take responsibility, it is also very freeing. When we change how we think, how we feel and what we do, it gives us the personal power to create new and better outcomes in our lives.

FALLACY OF FAIRNESS

The fallacy of fairness is when we believe that life is always supposed to be fair. When it isn't fair, we feel angry, cheated, or maybe even envious of others who seem to be having more luck.

An example would be when someone else gets a job that we

were interviewed for. We feel sure they got it because of their connections rather than their experience and qualities, and we feel resentful. Or, we develop a nasty illness and feel angry that we got it when we can think of lots of other people who deserved to suffer more!

Have you or someone you know been guilty of assuming that something would be fair, and getting angry or upset when it wasn't? What impact did that have?

Many of us have a very strong sense of fairness and justice, and believe that life should be equitable and fair. Yet when we look around us, it seems that life doesn't always work that way.

We can feel a greater sense of peace with the things that happen if we simply accept that things aren't always fair, and deal with them as best we can, trusting that everything is ultimately happening for our greater good (whether we can see it now, or not).

FALLACY OF CHANGE

We might believe that other people should change to suit us, and that if we work on, pressurise or cajole them enough, that we can change them.

It's based on the idea that our happiness stems from what the people around us do and don't do, rather than from our own thoughts, choices and actions. An example is someone being attracted to a 'bad boy' and believing that once they're married or have had children, he'll change and become good. Another example is a parent believing that if they shout at their child loudly enough or punish them in the right way, they'll get them to change a bad habit.

The truth is that the power to change lies only within the individual, and no-one else can do it for them. We can try and influence someone to change, but unless they're personally determined to do so, they won't change.

Have you ever tried to make someone change, or believed that you could? What did you do, and what was the result? We can frustrate and exhaust ourselves trying to change others when it's not even within our power. If you catch yourself thinking that you need someone to change in order to be happy, you're better off pondering what you could change with yourself or your own behavior, that would either enable you to feel better about the situation, or that might elicit a corresponding improvement in the other person. When we change, it's curious how others respond differently to us.

HEAVEN'S REWARD FALLACY

We tend to have an expectation that if we work hard and/or give selflessly to others, that we'll be rewarded for it. This is known as the 'Heaven's reward fallacy'.

We might, for example, do a lot of great work for charity, and believe this will act as insurance against bad things happening in our lives; or we might expect to receive praise and awards for the work that we do, and feel disappointed if our efforts seem to go unnoticed or unacknowledged - especially if an opportunity is given to someone else who doesn't appear to work as hard as we do.

Have you ever expected to be rewarded, and were disappointed when it didn't happen? That's just your natural sense of justice and fairness in operation.

Whilst it often follows that the harder we work, the 'luckier' we get, and the more good that we do, the more good comes back to us, there are, unfortunately, no guarantees in life. We should therefore aim to do what we do for the intrinsic pleasure and reward that it brings, rather than for external rewards or recognition. In this way, we can never feel disappointed or resentful, and any rewards that we get will be a lovely bonus.

SHOULDS

We tend to hold a lot of beliefs about what we and others should and shouldn't do, and how we should and shouldn't behave.

Different people from different backgrounds can have very different ideas about this. Some of these ideas are linked to laws and ethics, and can therefore be deemed reasonable; however, other ideas may be much more subjective, and are therefore not necessarily valid for everyone in all circumstances.

An example would be feeling that we should always exercise every day, and that we should never have treats (accompanied by feelings of pressure, and guilt/shame when we break our rules). Another example is believing that other people should always hold themselves up to the same standards and behaviours that we do, resulting in feelings of irritation, frustration and negative judgement when they don't.

What 'shoulds' do you place on yourself and others, and what effect do they have?

Try thinking in terms of 'coulds', rather than 'shoulds', offering more flexibility and choice (and we do always have a choice, even if it doesn't always feel that way).

Laws notwithstanding, it is best to simply accept that people are free to choose their own actions and behaviours (whilst not being free of the consequences of doing so).

CONFIRMATION BIAS

In life, we tend to see what we want to see, and disregard the rest. The tendency to search for, interpret, favour and recall information that confirms our existing beliefs is known as the 'confirmation bias'.

One example of this is that, whether we believe vaccines are safe or dangerous, we will tend not to search out evidence to the contrary. Another example would be preferring to spend time around people who think like we do, because their beliefs don't challenge our own. When we hear something about a subject that goes against (or even supports) what we know already, we can press the metaphorical 'I know' button in our minds and stop listening fully, thus blocking any potential new learning.

Can you think of a time when you've done this? It's very easy to think that you know all there is to know about something, and that you have nothing else to learn about it.

In situations where the validity of information is yet to be proven (or where research may have been biased), it's useful to ask ourselves: "Am I certain this is true?", "Have I considered all angles?", "What if it's wrong?" Remember that it's good to keep an open mind in most things, because much of what we 'know' is faulty, or at least only partially true.

THE HALO AND HORN EFFECTS

This is about evaluating someone's overall character based on one feature or aspect. In the halo effect, this might mean assuming that someone who looks good is good; in the horn effect, this might mean assuming that someone who doesn't look good isn't good.

An example of the halo effect is, when recruiting for a job, believing that the good looking, articulate and smartly dressed person is the best person for the job, based on those factors alone. An example of the horn effect is, when helping in a workplace investigation, believing that the employee accused of wrong-doing is probably guilty, based solely on their seeming caginess, or inability to make eye-contact.

Have you made these kinds of thinking errors in the past? What was the outcome of that?

Whilst appearances can give clues to character, it's dangerous to make assumptions. Better to ask yourself questions like: "Does this person have the skills, knowledge, experience, character (etc.) needed?"; "Could this be a decent person who's just lacking a few social skills?"; or "Is my overall perception being influenced by one characteristic? What else might I need to consider?"

STATUS QUO BIAS

This is not a preference for middle-aged men with long hair who wear denim! It's a preference for sticking with the way things are, rather than changing them - even when it's not in your (or everyone's) best interests to do so.

Examples include doing things the way you've always done them, even when there's an easier/better way; staying with an employer or partner when things are less than ideal, because "It's better the devil you know"; or even sticking with the same energy supplier or insurance provider year after year when there are significant gains to be made from switching.

Where might you be guilty of maintaining things as they are, rather than making changes that would benefit you and others? Is fear holding you back, or perhaps apathy, or something else?

If you catch yourself feeling inclined to maintain the status quo, ask yourself, "What do I have to lose and to gain, by a) keeping things as they are, and b) doing something else?". Many of us fear loss more than we welcome gain, so consider what it is you're afraid of losing, and how likely that is to really happen. Change generally tends to bring progress, and work in our favour.

GROUPTHINK

This is when a group or team of people are (or become) so similar in their outlook that they lose the ability to think in creative and divergent ways.

In this situation, a random divergent thinker may feel highly uncomfortable offering thoughts that go against the grain, hence perspectives can go unchallenged, meaning that outcomes become compromised.

Groupthink can lead to those involved believing that, because thinking within the group is in alignment, the proposed idea or decision must be right. It includes things like the unquestioning acceptance of what is popularly considered to be 'Best Practice' - even when it might not be.

When putting groups and teams together, it is tempting to choose people who we know will have things in common and who'll get along, when it's often more beneficial to seek out diversity and individuality - particularly regarding thinking styles. It's also essential to encourage employees to respectfully question, challenge and disagree with things they don't feel are right, and ensure there are no negative consequences to them for doing so.

SELF-SERVING BIAS

This is the tendency to give ourselves credit for our successes, but lay the blame for our failures on external causes. This enables us to maintain our self-esteem.

An example is hitting all our work targets for three months in a row, and putting it down to our hard work; we then fail to hit our target the following month, and put it down to market forces. Another example is getting a 'Good' rating in our workplace's annual review, and assuming it's because we're great at what we do; we then get a 'Satisfactory' rating the following year, and put it down to the new manager who we think doesn't like us.

When might you have blamed external forces for a result that you played a part in?

Most of us have a tendency towards the self-serving bias. Feeling good about our successes is healthy if we appreciate the other factors that contributed. However, if/when we catch ourselves blaming others or outside forces for a failure, we should ask ourselves how our own actions may have contributed. Nobody gets everything right all the time, and failure is a large part of how we learn. When we're honest with ourselves and mine our experiences for the learning that they hold, we rapidly improve and grow.

DUNNING-KRUGER EFFECT

This is a form of thinking distortion where we believe we're smarter or more competent at something than we really are. It's a kind of illusory superiority where we're unable (or perhaps unwilling) to see or accept our lack of ability.

Unconscious incompetence is the term used to describe the situation where we don't know what we don't yet know. Naturalist Charles Darwin is reported to have said that ignorance begets more confidence than knowledge!

An example is a young child assuming that he or she can ride a bike, when they haven't been taught yet, or a teenager thinking they can learn to drive in three lessons. Another example is those who've been managing people for years with no formal training thinking that they wouldn't benefit from some training. This may be part of the reason why 360° feedback surveys have been so popular in the workplace in recent decades!

Might there be some things that you're not so good at that other people see, but that you don't see yourself? Have you ever rejected feedback that your skills in a certain area weren't quite up to scratch? What if there was some truth in that? Would it benefit you to identify areas where a bit of training or coaching would be really beneficial?

We all have blind spots (you could say we're on the wrong side of our eyeballs!). Ask those that know you well for some feedback on what they think you could do better. Drop your defenses, in the knowledge that awareness of these things will help you begin to improve.

BANDWAGON EFFECT

This is the tendency to buy, do or believe things just because other people buy, do or believe the same. The more people there are doing something, the more inclined we are to jump on the bandwagon - regardless of the facts.

Fads and trends in America never take too long to filter over to those of us in the UK, and a similar effect can be seen between the UK and Australia. Celebrities are often paid a pile of money to be seen wearing or using a particular product, after which many people will rush out to buy the same thing, despite often absurd price-tags.

Gerry and Kate McCann may have fallen prey to the bandwagon effect when joining their friends on holiday in leaving their children to sleep unsupervised whilst they ate dinner nearby (whilst checking in on them periodically). The fact that other people that we know and respect are doing something can give us a sense of its acceptability and security, and could have led Gerry and Kate to assume that it would be safe to do the same, with the tragic result that their young daughter Madeleine was abducted.

I wonder how many of us have been influenced to do something that our friends were doing, that we would probably never have done otherwise. I suspect it's most of us. Have a think of a time when you might have hopped on a bandwagon, and with what effect.

We're all influenced by others, even if we don't realise it. We often wait to see what others do before taking action ourselves, and whilst this isn't always a bad thing, it can provide a false sense of security, because sometimes other people can be wrong.

When we feel inclined to jump on a bandwagon, it's helpful to check in with ourselves first, asking, "If no-one else was buying/doing/believing this, would I still want to?"

NEGATIVITY BIAS

Most, if not all of us, pay more attention and give more weight to information of a negative nature than that of a positive nature. It's to do with our survival instinct, and being on the alert for danger or anything that might prove to be a threat. Having an awareness of what *could* happen, somehow makes us feel more prepared and in control, if it *was* actually to happen.

One example of negativity bias is that 90% of the news presented by the media is negative, when this is not proportionately representative of reality. This is because we listen more to the negative than the positive, and therefore bad news sells more newspapers and attracts more viewers. Another example is remembering every insult we've ever received, whilst having forgotten most of the compliments.

Have you heard the black dot story?

One day, a professor asked his students to prepare for a surprise test. Once he'd handed the papers out face down, he asked the students to turn them over. To everyone's surprise, there were no questions – just a black dot in the centre of the paper.

The professor said: "I want you to write about what you see there." The students, a bit confused, got started on the task. At the end of the class, the professor took all the papers in and looked them over. All of them, with no exception, defined the black dot, explaining its position in the centre of the sheet.

The professor said: "I'm not going to grade you on this, I just wanted to give you something to think about. No one wrote about the white part of the paper. Everyone focused on the black dot – and the same thing happens in our lives. We insist on focusing on the black dot – the health issue, the lack of money, the complicated relationship, the disappointment with a friend. The dark spots are very small when compared to everything else in our lives, but they are the ones that pollute our minds. Take your eyes away from the black dots in your lives. Enjoy each one of your blessings, each moment that life gives you. Be happy and live a life filled with love!"

Where might you be aware of paying more attention to negatives than positives? If you catch yourself doing this, try asking yourself, "What are the positives in this [situation/person/thing] that I could choose to focus on instead?"; "Are things really as bad as I'm thinking or am I just dwelling on the negatives?"; "Is the larger part of my life pretty great, but I'm obsessing about one small aspect that isn't as I'd like it to be?"

That's not to say that we should ignore the negatives - just that it's helpful to see them in perspective, and approach them from a more constructive, solutions-focused mindset.

OPTIMISM BIAS

The optimism bias is where we overestimate the probability of positive events happening, and underestimate the probability of negative events. This includes believing that we are at a lesser risk of negative events, illness, etc. than other people are.

One example is continuing to smoke or eat badly because, "Cancer is something that happens to other people and not to me". Another example is not building in contingency time (or money) for things that might go wrong, because we think it's so unlikely that will happen.

Optimism feels much better than pessimism does. Believing that we're likely to succeed and that things will go well for us may lower our stress levels and lead to greater feelings of well-being. Many people believe that optimism increases the likelihood of good things happening through the law of attraction or power of the mind, and this might be true. However, it is possible to be too optimistic, and this could lead to poor risk management. We will probably all experience a mix of 'good' and 'bad' events in our lives, hence swapping blind optimism for a more balanced outlook could be more sensible.

Where might a healthy dose of balanced optimism (or realism) serve you well right now?

IN-GROUP BIAS

This is the tendency to trust and value people within our social circle (or those we perceive to be like us) more than we do other people.

As an example, cliques are commonplace, often side-lining those who they see as different. In the workplace this can create dysfunction, impacting on collaboration, performance and results. Outside of the workplace, some political and religious groups view other groups with distrust and dislike. These biases can lead to exclusion and discrimination, resulting in resentment and hatred. In the extreme, they can even result in terrorism.

Another example is when people from rival towns and cities are biased against people from their rival town.

Have you experienced or been involved in any in-group bias?

We can sometimes feel uncomfortable or unsafe with those we perceive to be different to us, when generally most people are good and trustworthy. Consider if you have a bias towards or against certain types of people, and how this might impact you, them and even the world at large. Experiment with getting to know people who are different to you. Despite our many differences, we are really all much the same.

ASSUMING THAT PERCEPTION IS REALITY

We think that what we see and hear is representative of how things really are. However, perception can be influenced by multiple factors, and we don't always see things as they really are, but rather, through our personal filters

Because 90% of news portrayed by the media is bad news, we may perceive that it's an unsafe world that we live in, and that there's no hope for mankind. In fact, we're probably safer now than we've ever been in history, and wonderful things are happening every day - they just aren't always reported in the news.

If most of our friends think similarly to us about political or other matters, this could lead us to believe that our thoughts are representative of the wider country. Election and referendum results can therefore be very surprising when it turns out that that wasn't the case.

Do you remember the fuss on social media some time ago over a gold/white and blue/black dress where different people saw different colours? There was also a similar thing with a voice recording where different people heard either the word 'Yanny' or 'Laurel'. Our brains literally perceive things differently, and who can truly say what's real and what's someone's faulty perception?

What misperceptions might you have experienced in life, and what impact did they have?

Perhaps we can't really be sure of the validity of anything we see, hear, read or think.

SUNK COST FALLACY

This is when we metaphorically 'throw good money after bad', thinking that further investment in something we've already invested time and/or money in, that hasn't delivered value, will magically make it do so.

Have you ever continued to watch a movie that has bored or annoyed you in the first 20 minutes, because you've invested time in it already and there's a chance it might improve? That's an example of the sunk-cost fallacy! Another example is holding on to clothes and items you will never use because you paid good money for them.

Early in the Concorde project, the sponsors reportedly realised it was going to lose a massive amount of money over its lifetime, but continued with it anyway. The sunk cost fallacy may have been a factor in their decision to carry on, or maybe they decided that the prestige and publicity of having such an aircraft would be worth it.

What examples of continuing to invest in something that's probably not going to deliver (and that's going to waste much more of your time, effort and/or money) might you have from your own life?

Loss aversion and fear of waste are two reasons that encourage us to keep investing in potentially lost causes. In these situations, consider how much worse you'll feel if at the end of the continued investment, something still pays no dividends.

Optimism in these situations may be misplaced, because if something has failed to deliver in the early stages, the chances of a miraculous turnaround are probably slim.

STORIES

Sometimes we take small pieces of information and tell ourselves a story about what they mean - otherwise known as putting two and two together and making five! This is about misunderstanding a situation, or putting our own spin on it - often (but not always) in a way that makes it bigger, worse or different than it actually was, and usually angling things so that we come out looking good, or innocent, or the victim.

The spin we put on things can link with our beliefs, our past experiences, or possibly to our identity narratives and life stories (as covered in Chapter 2). We mostly assume that these stories are true – not recognising that they're just tales that we're telling ourselves, or faulty assumptions and conclusions that we're making.

There are many kinds of stories that we tell ourselves, including:

- The boss wants to see me... I must have done something wrong!
- My child's late home from school... I hope they haven't had an accident!
- A friend hasn't answered my text straight away... I don't matter to them!
- I didn't get the job... I'm not good enough!
- I didn't get the date... I'm ugly and nobody loves me!
- It goes a bit quiet when I enter the room... They were talking about me!
- I've got a strange rash... It must be meningitis!
- He's late again... He doesn't respect my time!
- She's always so rude... She clearly doesn't like me!
- He's started to take more care in his appearance... he's having an affair!
- There's absolutely nothing I can do in this situation.

- He's just an evil person. There's no point trying to rationalise with him.
- She's a lazy 'good-for-nothing'!
- I could never...
- He/she always...
- I guess I'm too...
- I just don't have the time.
- I'm not ready.
- I'm just not a creative person.

This list is just the tip of the iceberg. You will no doubt have your own unique brand of stories. The danger is that when filling in the blanks, we confuse our stories, assumptions and conclusions with facts.

The next time you tell yourself anything similar to the above, catch yourself, and ask yourself what the facts are. Then consider if you could be deleting, distorting, generalising or otherwise making up a story that might not be true. Consider what else the situation could mean. It's like holding your thoughts up to scrutiny rather than assuming that just because you think something, it must therefore be true.

These are just a few of the many different types of thinking errors, distortions and biases that we can be prone to. It's quite an interesting study, and there's a lot of information freely available online (although take care to use reliable sources). You might like to start by investigating the Cognitive Bias Codex, which contains around 200 different listings:

https://commons.wikimedia.org/wiki/File:Cognitive_bias_codex _en.svg.

CHAPTER 4 SUMMARY

✓ Most people can think of a time when they thought about something too much, for too long, and disproportionately to the situation. Consistent over-thinking, though, is a symptom of anxiety, and is exhausting and unhelpful. It steals our joy and keeps us stuck. We spend too much time up in our heads thinking (maybe ruminating on something that's happened, or worrying about something that might happen), and not enough time in the moment, engaging with our senses and with what's currently happening. Talking about our concerns, or writing them down, helps us to work through them and see them in perspective.

✓ Worry, fear and doubt afflict us all sometimes, but most of the bad things that we imagine, never happen. Whilst a small amount of focus on the things that might go wrong can be helpful (for example in contingency planning, keeping us safe from genuine threats, and keeping us humble), too much thought in this direction can rob us of our joy and peace. A lot of things are uncertain in life, but ultimately – whether we worry about them or not - we can't control most of them. Best to relax and let go, trusting in ourselves and in the process of life to keep us safe and well.

✓ Criticism isn't generally helpful. Constructive feedback is. Don't criticise yourself or others.

✓ If you want to be happy, avoid comparing yourself with others. There will always be people who are better and worse than you in some things, or who have less or more than you do. We are all just different. Make the best of who you are and be happy.

✓ Our thoughts can sometimes jump about, as we make connections from one idea to another – sometimes going off on tangents. We can become unfocused and scattered in our thinking, particularly when trying to do more than one thing at a time. The busier we are, the worse this can get, and the greater the likelihood of making an error or dropping a metaphorical ball or plate. Mindfulness practice, and dealing with one thing at a time can help us become more focused, as can switching off alerts on our phones and emails.

✓ We don't always see things as they really are because we perceive them through the filters of our experience and our 'programming'. We are all, therefore, subject to perception errors and faulty thinking. Understanding the specific errors that we are personally prone to making can help us become more conscious of them when they're happening, giving us the opportunity to question their validity and stop them in their tracks.

"WE CAN CHANGE THE WORLD IF WE CHANGE OURSELVES. WE JUST NEED TO GET HOLD OF THE PATTERNS OF THINKING AND DEALING WITH THINGS, AND START LISTENING TO OUR INNER VOICES AND TRUSTING OUR SUPERPOWERS"

- NINA HAGAN -

Chapter 5

OUR THINKING CAN BE OUR SUPERPOWER

So far, this book has covered many of the ways in which our thinking can be unhelpful and dysfunctional. However, there are many ways in which our thinking can be positive, constructive and transformational in our lives. This chapter explores several of them, to help you re-train your thinking into being your superpower rather than your Kryptonite – most of the time, at least!

STEERING YOUR SHIP

As we learned in Chapter 1, our thoughts create our experiences. The Buddha is quoted as having said, "Your worst enemy cannot harm you as much as your own thoughts, unguarded. But once mastered, no one can help you as much, not even your father or your mother."

Much of the time, unless we've trained ourselves otherwise, our thinking is likely to be happening outside of our conscious control, like a vehicle in auto-pilot mode, with thoughts coming and going largely outside of our conscious awareness.

Whilst this isn't necessarily a problem (for instance, when our thinking has a positive/constructive theme), it can create problems for us (for instance, when our thinking has a negative/unhelpful theme).

Sometimes, the lower, more fearful part of our mind needs a bit of help from the higher, more loving part where our awareness sits, to keep us on course to creating the kind of positive outcomes that we want, and steer us away from creating the kind of negative outcomes that we don't want.

I like to use the analogy of a captain at the wheel of his or her ship, steering and course-correcting as needed. This is about taking greater directorship of ourselves, and switching our thinking from auto-pilot mode to manual, so that we're consciously choosing the kind of thoughts and actions that will help us to reach our desired destination, and help us avoid getting caught up in the seaweed, or in dangerous territory.

When our thoughts are left unchecked, they can drift in unhelpful directions that stir up anxiety and other difficult emotions which can cause negative, unhelpful actions and behaviours. When this happens, we need to catch ourselves in the act, and consciously switch into manual mode where we are more aware, intentional and purposeful in our thoughts and actions, thus steering our ship in the direction we wish to go.

Whilst it might be a nice aspiration to be in manual mode all the time, aware of and directing our thoughts, feelings and actions/behaviours, I'm not sure how realistic that is for most of us. Whilst it might potentially be possible (I expect the Buddha and other enlightened masters achieved it!), my feeling is that it's sometimes good to let go and enjoy a bit of down-time. On that basis, the particular occasions when I believe manual mode is of most help to us, include:

- When we're in meetings and communication with others
- When we catch ourselves thinking fear, worry and/or doubt-based thoughts (we might notice the subsequent emotions first)
- When we feel tensions or emotions beginning to rise in ourselves or others
- At the beginning, end, and in the middle of something - for example a day, a project, a piece of work, and so on, to ensure we are focusing our minds appropriately (I've included the end because of the usefulness of proper reflection).

Where the mind goes, the body follows. This means consciously thinking about what we want to achieve, then looking at what we need to do to bring that about. In this way, we are creating and responding to events rather than simply reacting to them.

Taking directorship – steering the ship - means posing questions to ourselves regularly in order to keep us on track. The specific questions will depend on the situation, but may include some of the following:

- What do I/we want, why, and what's most important to me/us?

- Is my/our current path and habits going to get me/us there? If not, what needs to change?
- What do I/we want to achieve today / this week / this month / this year / in 5 years' time?
- What are the priorities?
- What will need to happen first, then second (etc)?
- What's the best, most efficient and effective way of doing this?
- Who's help will I/we need?
- What could derail me/us, and how will I/we deal with these things?
- How can I/we stay focused, no matter what?
- How am I/are we feeling (physically, mentally, emotionally and in my / our spirits)?
- What are the thoughts that are causing these feelings?
- What situations are inspiring these thoughts, and what can I/we do about them (if needed)?
- What assumptions and judgements am I/are we making, and could I/we be wrong?
- What is going well?
- What is not going so well?
- What do I need to say and/or do now to get things back on track?
- Do I/we need to 'course-correct'?
- What needs to change, and how?
- What is the real problem I/we are facing, and is this just a symptom of a deeper problem?
- What's causing that to happen, and why?

- Have I/we lost sight of our purpose?
- Am I/are we getting caught up in the weeds, or overlooking important details?
- What have I/we learned that I/we will/won't repeat?

This is not an exhaustive list but should provide an idea of the kind of directive thinking that's needed in some of the situations mentioned. The quality of questions we ask determines the quality of the insights we get, and the results we achieve. Becoming conscious of, and directing our thoughts - especially in the kind of scenarios mentioned earlier - is an important skill for happiness and success in life. It doesn't mean that we should try and control everything all the time – just that we should step up into greater directorship when it's required, keeping our ship on course for the desired destination.

RIGHT-THINKING

Right-thinking in this context refers to the wholesomeness, clarity and morality of our thoughts. For example, someone who is experiencing clear, cogent, sane and rational thoughts, and upholding commonly held moral principles, could be said to be right-thinking. They're not falling foul of any thinking errors, and are holding appropriate convictions and beliefs.

The Buddhist 'Noble Eightfold Path' contains a number of themes related to right-thinking. Whilst there seem to be subtly different versions and variations on what the paths are called, a popular version includes the following:

- **Right thought** – thought that's consciously directed rather than wandering, and that's wholesome and constructive. Right thought relates to:
  - Thoughts of non-attachment (to the desire for things, people, concepts)
  - Thoughts of love, compassion and non-violence toward all beings
  - Thoughts of helpfulness.
- **Right understanding** (or right view) – dropping our illusions and perceiving things as they are in their true nature. Understanding that we are connected with all living things. Knowing that our actions have consequences, and we create our own reality. Accepting what is, knowing that what arises will also cease. Understanding that happiness, contentment, joy, suffering, anguish and despair come from thoughts rather than circumstances themselves – however it might seem.
- **Right concentration** – focusing the mind without distraction (developable through meditation).
- **Right mindfulness** – being fully present, maintaining a calm awareness of body, mind, feelings, and of the outside world.

When we adopt right-thinking, we're almost assured of a right-outcome, in accordance with the law of karma (which in Buddhist understanding means cause and effect).

GLORIOUS THINKING

We always have a choice about what to think. While our thoughts generally tend to run on autopilot, we can, at any moment, choose to take control and switch into manual mode, directing them in any ways we choose.

Oscar Wilde once wrote, "We are all in the gutter, but some of us are looking at the stars." I take this to mean that we're all here on this planet, having these human experiences and dealing with our problems and challenges as they arise. We can either place all of our attention on the problems and challenges, or we can elevate our perspective and focus on what we want instead – a brighter, better future. This doesn't necessarily mean that we should avoid thinking about our problems – just that when we do, the focus shouldn't be, "Woe is me... what a terrible situation this is," but rather, "What needs to change, what are my options and where can I get some advice, help and support?"

Author and healer Louise Hay once said, "Think glorious thoughts and you will have a glorious future." In this context, I take the word glorious to mean wonderful, beautiful, loving, expansive, exciting and inspiring thoughts. When we think these kinds of thoughts, we generate a high-vibrational energy within us that makes us feel great. When we feel great, this perpetuates and reinforces the glorious thoughts, making us much more resourceful and positive in our actions.

Whilst talk of raising vibrations can sound a bit 1967 (the 'summer of love' and height of the hippy movement), it is in fact scientific. Quantum physics has demonstrated that everything in the universe consists of tiny particles of energy, all vibrating at different frequencies. Physicist Dr David R. Hawkins was able to measure the vibratory frequency of different states of consciousness and emotion, and found that peace, joy and love are amongst the highest vibrational emotions, with hopelessness, guilt and shame being amongst the lowest. The law of attraction states that whatever vibrational frequency our thoughts and feelings are generating at, we magnetically draw towards us that which is of a similar vibration – thus, when we're experiencing positive emotions, more good seems to come to us, and when we're experiencing negative emotions, more bad seems to come to us. As engineer and inventor Nikola Tesla said, "If you want to find the secrets of the universe, think in terms of energy, frequency and vibration." We attract as we think and feel, or receive as we give.

Whilst life is never going to be perfect by our definition, we probably all have reasons to be joyful – we just tend to take many of them for granted. When we think glorious thoughts (for example, about who we love and what we're thankful for), when we're playful and joyful, and when we think peaceful thoughts, we generate wonderful feelings that lift us (and others) up. From these powerful, high-vibrational frequencies, we are far better able to create the kind of results and outcomes that we want – perhaps particularly so when those things benefit the greater good of all. A high vibe brings great power to our magnetism, and our manifestation efforts.

Whilst thoughts create feelings, feelings also influence thoughts, and there are lots of things we can do to raise our feeling frequency, in order to inspire glorious thoughts. These include listening to good music, reading inspiring literature, taking walks in the fresh air and sunshine, swimming in the sea, meditating, practicing yoga, playing the "Wouldn't it be cool if..." game (where we think about all the good we'd like to create in our lives, and make ourselves feel really excited about those things), to name just a few – any of which can be woven into a daily routine.

Try the following exercise the next time you need a lift:

- Go to a quiet place where you won't be disturbed, and switch off all media. Outdoors is ideal if you have a quiet-ish environment; otherwise, opening a window is good - assuming there isn't a motorway or noisy construction work going on outside!
- Sit comfortably with your back straight if you can, and your feet flat on the floor. Close your eyes and take a deep but comfortable breath in, then let it go. Consciously take control of your breathing throughout this exercise, breathing in deeply and comfortably, then letting it go at a pace that feels good to you. Feel your system becoming oxygenated, and notice that you're beginning to feel calmer and better (signalling that your vibe is already rising!).
- Get a sense of your physical body... your feet on the ground... your bum in the chair... and notice if there's any tension anywhere in your body (especially check the muscles in your bum, stomach, neck, shoulders and face), and allow them to let go and relax.
- Feel the play and temperature of the air on your skin. Notice any scents around you. Bask in the awareness of your senses, and feel your vibe rising even more. Notice

the corners of your mouth feeling relaxed and wanting to turn ever so gently upward.

- Now think of all the great people in your life, and all the wonderful qualities that they have. Silently (or out loud, if preferred) say thank you for each one: "*Thank you for Max and his love, support and hugs... Thank you for Joe and his amazing way of seeing the world and knowing what people are thinking... Thank you for Edd, for his strength, his warmth, and his love... Thank you for Nacho, for his soft fur and zen-like purr... Thank you for my girlfriends, for their company, fun and laughter*"... and so on. Feel the love that you have for them, and the love that comes back to you.

- Now think of yourself, and all the things about you that are wonderful and that you're grateful for. Name them and say thank you for each one: "Thank you for a strong and healthy body that responds so readily to what I put in it... Thank you for the self-healing mechanism that allows my body to heal, repair and rejuvenate when I provide the right conditions for it to do so... Thank you for the strong legs that carry me wherever I want to go... Thank you for the magic within me that has grown, fed and nurtured my beautiful children... Thank you for this face, these features and this hair that I sometimes battle with, but am grateful I still have!... Thank you for my sensitivity and strength..., for my kindness and my goodness, and the deep well of love that I have, that sustains me and others"... and so on.

- Now think about every good thing in your life and the benefits they bring. Again, name them and say thank for each one: "Thank you for this beautiful planet that we live on that sustains us in every way possible... Thank you for my lovely home, and the safe and peaceful neighbourhood I live in... Thank you for my warm and comfortable bed, and the hours of deep and restful sleep it offers... Thank you for the rain that keeps things green and growing... Thank you for the sun that warms my bones and brightens up my days... Thank you for the water that's there whenever I turn the tap on... Thank you for my car which takes me anywhere I want, safely and reliably... Thank you for the food that's so freely available at the shops and markets... Thank you to the workers that clean the water, grow the food, drive the trucks, stock the shelves"... and so on. Feel the gratitude that you have for everything in your life that enables you to do what you do. Get a sense of how fortunate you are, and how easy life is for you in so many ways.

- Get a sense that you are connected to everyone and everything in the universe (maybe even to something bigger than humanity – to 'God', or a higher power that holds everything in perfect order (despite any appearances to the contrary). See that, despite our differences, we are all made of the same stuff... that we're all having similar experiences that we're learning and growing from... all having our struggles, our successes, our highs and our lows. Realise that this is not a competition – that we are here to help and support one another... that we thrive collectively, not independently. Picture a future for humankind where most people live consciously, and maintain positive emotional states.

Recognise the magical power of your mind to help create this new reality.

- Set an intention to notice all the little things you have to be grateful for, at any moment during the day – for electricity when boiling the kettle... for the cows or the plants that provide the milk, and so on. Don't reserve your gratitude for exercises like this, and when something goes wrong (annoying though it can be), appreciate the fact that most of the time, it goes right ☺.

COURAGE, SELF-CONFIDENCE AND SELF-ESTEEM

Courage and self-confidence are interlinked. Courage is a kind of mental strength that enables us to do the things that scare us. Self-confidence is a belief in our abilities and qualities. It comes from stepping out of our comfort zones, and trying new things.

Self-esteem is how we regard ourselves, based on the value we believe we have. We pick up these ideas about our value in our early lives, based largely on how we're treated by those around us, and this can be unconsciously reinforced in later life through what we accept and disallow.

Many of us lack a bit of confidence in certain situations, and we probably all carry a few fears that can cause us to stay safe and play small. However, feelings of courage, confidence and self-esteem are strongly influenced by our thoughts, so if we want to experience more of these strong, positive feelings, we can achieve that by changing our thoughts, and slowly and progressively doing some of the things that scare us.

Writer Mark Twain is quoted to have said, "I've had a lot of worries in my life, most of which never happened." This seems to be true - most of our fears never happen, and even when they do, it's rarely as bad as we anticipated it might be. When trying to find the courage to do something, it can first be helpful to identify:

- What, specifically, we're worried might happen
- How likely it really is that it could happen
- What the impact would be if it happened.

If there's a good chance that something bad would happen, and it would truly be devastating if it did, then it would be reasonable not to do it; but more usually there's a relatively low chance of something going wrong. Even if it did, we'd probably be embarrassed for a short period of time before getting over it and moving on. There is often something we can do to minimise the risk involved in an activity, and put a contingency plan in place for that eventuality.

Fears tend to disappear when we face them head on. They are only ideas and chemicals after all!

Courage is necessary if we wish to break out of our self-imposed boundaries and make progress in life. Failure may well be a possible outcome, but it's a necessary part of the learning process sometimes, and it really doesn't matter that much. Feel the fear and do it anyway, as author Susan Jeffers said so beautifully and simply in her book of the same title!

Schools are now teaching children that FAIL stands for 'First Attempt In Learning'. As novelist and playwright Samuel Beckett said, "Ever tried? Ever failed? No matter. Try again. Fail again. Fail better." Just doing something and accepting that you might fail (and feeling ok about it) is very freeing, and best of all, it helps to build our confidence muscle. What's the worst that could happen, and what do you have to gain? Weigh up the risks and benefits rationally, and if it all adds up, go for it. As super-brand Nike says: 'Just do it' (or 'JFDI', as some people prefer!).

While you're at it, tell yourself that you're a courageous person ("Ah, what the heck?! I'm a courageous, 'Feel the fear and do it anyway' kind of person. You only live once").

Self-confidence is built on the back of courage. It goes like this: Have courage > take action > succeed > feel good about yourself (or maybe: Have courage > take action > don't get it right first time but have another go, and maybe another > then succeed > then feel really good about yourself!).

Making a list of everything you've ever done that once seemed a bit frightening but is now much less so, is a good reminder of how easy it is to build competence and confidence. Many things are a bit scary the first time we do them, from riding a bike, learning to drive, learning to swim, giving a presentation, diving into a pool, asking someone out on a date, asking for a pay rise, telling someone you're not happy with something they're doing and you want it to stop it, and so on.

Have a think about some things that you used to find scary, that you don't anymore (or maybe you still do a bit, but you crack on anyway). Write them down:

How much more confident would you like to be a year from now? Which of the things that frighten you today would you like to face head-on and overcome, between now and then? Jot your priority things down now:

_____

_____

_____

_____

_____

_____

_____

_____

_____

_____

Now, using the visualisation technique described in Chapter 3, imagine yourself doing each of these things as clearly as you can, and enjoying doing so. Especially, imagine how amazing you'll feel having done them, and the massive uplift in confidence you'll experience. Repeat this exercise often, and ask life to provide the perfect opportunities for you to try these things in a safe and supported way. As Pooh bear once famously said to Piglet, "You're braver than you believe, stronger than you seem and smarter than you think!".

Self-esteem comes from believing positive things about ourselves. If we've been bullied, teased, abused or subjected to prejudice and discrimination, the chances are that our self-esteem might be low. Maybe you had a critical parent or person in your life at some stage, whose behaviour and treatment of you lead you to believe that you weren't good enough.

It can be helpful to think about the names we've been called, the negative messages we've picked up about ourselves from others, and the assumptions and conclusions we've made about ourselves over the years, and to recognise that these are unlikely to be true. They're only words and thoughts in reality – nothing more – and they do not define you. However, if you take them on board and believe them, they become as powerful as if they were real.

The following exercise is recommended only if your mental and emotional health is generally good, and you feel reasonably strong. Read it through first and if you feel any concerns about doing it, I would suggest you either bypass it altogether, defer it to such a time when you're feeling stronger, or work with a therapist so you're supported whilst doing it.

Allocate a good time when you can be alone in a quiet, safe environment, and recall every unkind name you've ever been called, every negative message you've ever picked up about yourself, and every negative assumption you've ever made about yourself, and write these down on a piece of paper. Notice how you feel as you do it. If you feel strong emotions surfacing, allow them to come up and be expressed so that you can feel them, breathe through them and release them. Know that any emotional pain that surfaces is temporary, that you can manage it, and that it will pass. When you've completed your list, look through it again and say to yourself:

- "(Your name), I'm sorry that you've experienced these things, but they're nothing more than thoughts and words you may have heard, thought or believed. It's not your fault, and I understand why you might have been feeling or thinking badly about yourself.
- I know you've been working hard to deal with this stuff, and forgive me for not always being present and listening to you. Forgive me for ever believing any of this might be true, and for any times when I may have judged or criticised you.
- Thank you for bravely getting on with life despite everything you've been through. Thank you for being the amazing, courageous person that you are, despite everything.
- I love you. Every part of you is wonderful just as it is, and you deserve all the good that life has to offer. Please wake up to the truth, and let go of the lies and faulty beliefs. Realise your true nature and potential.

Once done, you can do whatever you wish with the piece of paper, but I would recommend being dramatic and ceremonious! You could choose to burn it, deface it, shred it, screw it up and chuck it in the bin, bury it, send it out to sea, or whatever you fancy. This sends a powerful message that you have let that stuff go, and are ready to move on.

You may have noticed that this exercise follows the pattern of Ho'oponopono mentioned earlier in the book. You might also like to check out the work of spiritual healer and author Tara Love Perry, and her book *I Love You, Me – 7 Steps to Transformational Self-love*, which describes a beautiful and deeply moving process that follows a similar pattern.

Take a bit of time now to think about all the things about yourself that are good and wonderful, and write these down. If it feels hard, think about every lovely compliment you've ever received and turn each into an "I am….." or "I have….." type of statement. See if you can fill up the space here, and if you need more, continue on another piece of paper. Write down as much stuff as you possibly can.

_____

_____

_____

_____

_____

_____

_____

_____

_____

_____

_____

_____

To follow are several visualisation techniques you can use when someone's making things difficult for you, or otherwise sending negativity your way:

- Imagine yourself with an invisible forcefield all around you. This forcefield lets in positive energy, love, and so on, but it bounces off negative energy, insults and harsh/unkind words, so that they can't get in and hurt you;

- If there's name calling or unpleasant words coming your way, see them leaving the person's mouth as written words that mean nothing, and that fall to the ground as a pile of individual letters well before reaching you. They're not real or true, and they can't hurt you unless you take on their energy. Stubbornly refuse to take in anyone's negative energy;

- Imagine that you're surrounded by a titanium suit of armour that's indestructible, and that you can't be hurt or harmed. Feel how strong and invincible you are, inside and out;

- Imagine filling yourself up with so much love (picture a hot pink substance, or whatever works for you) or energy (picture sparkling yellow light, or similar) that you radiate positive, loving energy for two metres in every direction around you. This energy can't help but influence the people nearby, so not only can negativity not get to you, but you can positively transform it into love, or peace, or neutrality - whatever the people around you are able to assimilate.

Visualise yourself in past and/or future scenarios using these techniques to good effect. Feel how good it feels to be strong; to bounce things off; to feel great; to feel loved no matter what. In fact, when we know that we're wonderful, talented, loveable human beings, nothing and no-one can hurt us. It's like we're so solid on the inside that there's no room for anything else.

REFRAMING

This is the simple act of looking at something (a situation, person, relationship, etc) from a different perspective in order to see it in a different light, and perhaps to feel better about it.

I remember in my neuro-linguistic programming (NLP) training years ago bemoaning the challenging behaviour of my son, who was a toddler at the time. Groups of us had to get into a circle and state something that had been annoying us, getting us down or similar, then the others in the group had to take it in turns to reframe the situation.

I said something about how my son had been behaving like a complete little sh*t and had been doing my head in! Cue lots of people telling me how lucky I was to even have a child, and to have one that was so clearly sparky and knew his own mind!

Maybe there's a positive (or silver lining) in every negative, if we look for it – as is the case in the story of the very old lady...

A very old lady looked in the mirror one morning. She had three remaining hairs on her head, and being a positive soul, she said, "I think I'll braid my hair today." So, she braided her three hairs and she had a great day.

Some days later, looking in the mirror one morning and preparing for her day, she saw that she had only two hairs remaining. "Hmm" she said, "two hairs... I fancy a centre parting today." She duly parted her two hairs and as ever, she had a great day.

A week or so later, she saw that she had just one hair left on her head. "One hair huh...," she mused, "I know, a pony-tail will be perfect." And again, she had a great day.

The next morning, she looked in the mirror and found she was completely bald. "Finally, bald huh?" she said to herself, "How wonderful! I won't have to waste time doing my hair any more..."

What situations are you experiencing in your life that could be reframed or turned around to your advantage?

SOLUTION FOCUS

Thoughts are the building blocks of creation. They literally shape our world and mould our experiences, so it's of the utmost importance that we keep our thinking trained on the outcomes that we want, and not those we don't want.

'Solution focus' is a thinking approach that enables us to quickly create solutions rather than dwelling on problems.

When faced with a difficult challenge or problem, many of us will find ourselves ruminating on the situation, thinking thoughts along the lines of:

- "This is so hard. I can't see how I'm going to overcome this."

- "Why me? Why now? Man, this sucks!"
- "I hate it when things like this happen. Why is nothing ever straight-forward?"
- "Oh, great! Because we really need this kind of hassle right now, don't we?!"
- "Oh no... this is terrible. What if lots of other bad things happen too... like what if I get sick, and what if we run out of money, and what if it all turns to crap and we fail and lose everything?"
- "I don't think I can do this. I can't do it. I don't have the strength for it. I've never been very good at this. I'm so scared. I feel sick. Maybe I should go and lie down for a bit!"
- "I just can't see a solution to this problem. Maybe there isn't one – maybe we should give up now."

In all these cases, the thinker is picturing something they don't want. They're seeing the problem, the obstacle, their perceived shortcomings, the inconvenience, failure, doom, and so on. They are, in fact, envisioning the exact opposite of what they want, and are thereby planting seeds of failure rather than success.

Whilst magic solutions can't always be found, there is usually a way forward if we place our thoughts in the right direction. This requires first accepting the belief or principle that we all have within us the means and resources to deal with whatever life presents us with.

When adopting solution focus, instead of allowing worries, fears, doubts and catastrophic thoughts to dominate, we think in terms of what we want instead, and what we can do to achieve it. The thoughts might go something like this:

- "This situation will be quickly resolved, and normal life will continue."
- "I/we have all the means and inner resources needed to overcome this."
- "I/we picture the situation now with a satisfying outcome – every aspect resolved."
- "What are all the different actions I/we could potentially take that would make a difference to this situation?"
- "What have I/we/others done before in a similar situation that's helped us to succeed?"
- "Of these things, which do I/we believe could work for me/us, and that I'm/we're prepared and able to do?"
- "Will I/we need any help, and if so, from whom?"
- "What's the first step, and the second (and so on)…?"
- "I/we've got this. I/we've met every challenge so far, and will meet this one too."

Then just stay focused on your desired outcome, whilst continuing to take all necessary actions. If you catch yourself diverting back to unhelpful thinking, say, "You're not helping me" to those thoughts, and then visualise yourself throwing them on the scrap heap and reaching for a better, more solution focused thought.

APPRECIATIVE INQUIRY

In its broadest sense, 'Appreciative Inquiry' is an improvement model used in organisational development to identify what's working well, in order to do more of it and improve performance.

Appreciative inquiry in the context of this book is a strengths-based approach to searching for the best in people and situations, in order to accentuate and maximise the positives (remembering that we tend to get what we focus on).

We are evolving in many ways from a society whose focus in the past was substantially on faults, criticism, blame, distrust, etc., to a much more positive focus on strengths, appreciation, gratitude and trust.

Parents and managers take note: people (and situations) have a habit of living up, or down, to our expectations of them, depending on whether our expectations are positive, in which case the person or situation will tend to rise up to them, or whether our expectations are negative, in which case the person or situation will tend to live down to them. When we look for the good and focus on what we can appreciate, we tend to get more of that. When we look for the bad and focus on what we can find fault with, we tend to get more of that. By side-stepping our tendency to focus on the negatives, and consciously choosing to adopt an approach of appreciate inquiry, our experience of people and situations can totally turn around. As poet and playwright William Shakespeare once said, "There is nothing either good or bad, but thinking makes it so."

An appreciative inquiry might include asking ourselves the following kinds of questions:

- "What's positive about (XXXXX)?"
- "What strengths do I notice in (XXXXX)?"

- "What could I choose to appreciate about (XXXXX)?"
- "What am I grateful for about (XXXXX)?"
- "How can I help or develop (XXXXX)?"

Think of a person or situation that you experience as bad or difficult. What if it isn't so much that the person or situation is bad, but rather that something in your thinking makes you experience them that way – after all, there may be others who speak positively about that person or situation.

Whilst saying this, I do know that there are some people and situations that are experienced by most, if not all people, as difficult, horrible, and so on. It's just that, without our thoughts and judgements, we wouldn't even be experiencing those feelings. That might be where the somewhat annoying* saying, "It is what it is" comes from (*note: 'annoying' is a subjective judgement and feeling in itself!). Nothing can be experienced as good or bad without the judgement of our thinking. Perhaps my annoyance with this saying comes from the fact that it can sometimes be used as an excuse not to change something that's changeable!

The next time you experience a critical thought about a person or situation, ask yourself:

- "What feelings do I have about (XXXXX)?"
- "What thoughts have I been thinking about (XXXXX) that created these feelings?"
- "What stories do I tell myself about (XXXXX)?"
- "Am I choosing to focus only on the negatives?"
- "What positives would I find if I really looked for them?"
- "What else could I find to appreciate about (XXXXX)?"

- "What might happen if I trained myself to think differently about (XXXXX)?" (Even if you can't find any positives, you could at least choose to let go of judgements).
- "What other benefits might there be?"
- "Am I willing to change my thinking in order to experience a different reality?"

Make an experiment of this. See if you can turn around a difficult or annoying experience just by changing your thoughts, and focusing on what you could appreciate instead.

QUESTIONS ARE THE ANSWER

Our brains are like computers. Present them with a problem and they can't really do anything; however, present them with a question and they will go off on a little search to come up with some answers.

When we feel stuck or are experiencing a problem, it does no good to focus on the feeling of being stuck, or on the problem itself. The best thing we can do to help ourselves move forward is to change our thinking. Sometimes this can be achieved by another person asking us a question that gets us thinking along different lines. In the absence of a handy person or coach though, there are certain questions we can ask ourselves that can help unlock some answers.

The quality of the answers that come to us will always depend on the quality of the questions that we ask. Open questions are amongst the most useful, and may begin with the following words:

- Who
- What
- Where
- When
- Why
- How

All of these have a place in different scenarios but the "What…?" and "How…?" questions are often the most useful, and the "Why…?" questions are useful only when they come from a place of genuine curiosity and seeking to understand (as opposed to "Why am I so stupid?!" or "Why are things so difficult?", etc., which serve no constructive purpose).

As Einstein is reported to have said, "No problem can be solved by the same kind of thinking that created it."

To follow are some questions we can ask ourselves when we're feeling stuck:

- "What do I really want, that I feel is currently lacking?"
- "Why do I want it? What benefits do I think it will bring?"
- "Am I sure what I want will bring those benefits? Is there an easier way to get those things?"
- "What would I benefit from starting to do, or doing more of?"
- "What have I been avoiding doing that would move me forward?"

- "What's holding me back from achieving my goals? Is there something I need to stop doing?"
- "What will happen if I don't take action?"
- "Who is good for me in my life? Who isn't good for me? Do I need to make some changes?"
- "Would I benefit from learning new skills, or investing in new resources?"
- "Who can help me move forwards?"

To follow are some questions we can ask ourselves when faced with a problem:

- "What, specifically, is the problem/situation?"
- "Is this the 'real' problem, or is it a symptom of a deeper problem? If so, what?"
- "What's good about the problem? Is there an opportunity to create something better here?"
- "What has led to the problem (i.e. what are the facts)?"
- "Why have these things happened (i.e. what are the drivers/root causes)?"
- "What suppositions, assumptions, judgements, etc. might I have made, or be making?"
- "Where is more love needed?" (Whatever the problem, love, or caring, is usually part of the answer)
- "What outcome do I want to achieve (that's in everyone's best interests)?"
- "How can I begin to resolve the problem?"
- "What do I need to do first, second (and so on)?"
- "When is the best time to carry out these actions?"

- "Where is the best place to carry out these actions?"
- "Who's help might I need?"
- "What else might be possible once the problem has been solved?"
- "How can I share this learning, and with whom?"

Outcomes that aren't in the best interests of all concerned come at a high cost. Always aim to reach win/win outcomes that everyone involved can be happy with, or accepting of.

Many problems stem from a lack of love. Problems occur when we don't love and accept ourselves and others in the way that we perhaps should. There's no getting away from it - until we can find a way of staying centred in positive, loving thoughts and feelings, we will always create and experience problems.

I once heard the saying, "The people who are the hardest to love are the ones that need our love the most." This is a massive challenge for many human beings, especially when some people, on the face of it, are nasty, hateful, even 'evil'. Maybe we feel that they deserve our judgement and hatred; however, when we judge, hate and criticise others, we are also hurting and poisoning ourselves. Our bodies receive every thought that we think, and produce chemicals and emotions in response. Love is the only power that can transform hate. It's possible to accept and love the essence of a person (the divine spark that's within them and everyone) without condoning or approving of their behaviour.

Who are the people that you find hard to love (or that you catch yourself judging and criticising a lot)?

Try sending them love instead. Try telling yourself a different story about them – maybe that they're the way they are because of what they've been taught, or the things they've been through. Then see what happens. It's a little bit of magic.

THINKING TOOLS

There are many tools available that can aid our thinking. None of them appear revolutionary, but they can really help to guide our thinking in a logical and sequential way, so that we consider all relevant aspects of a situation in a way that we probably wouldn't if we were left to our own devices.

To follow are a few thinking tools and models that might prove useful to you.

MIND MAPPING

Mind mapping is a brilliant visual tool that can help in all sorts of thinking including organising information, studying and the brainstorming or planning of an event, meetings, speech, presentations, workshops, books, reports, assignments, dissertations, and so on. Essentially, you start out with a central theme on a piece of paper and then add large theme branches followed by sub themes coming off these branches and so on. You can colour code and add illustrations if you like or keep them basic - depending on your purpose. You can draw them freehand or use mind-mapping software, of which there are plenty of options online including some free basic models.

CREATIVE PROBLEM SOLVING

This is a 6-step process for problem solving in which you work your way through each step sequentially, as follows:

1. **Objective Finding** – "What's the problem, and what's my/our objective?"
2. **Fact Finding** – "What are the facts? What do I/we know for sure?"
3. **Problem Finding** – "What are the specific problems, and what's causing them?"
4. **Idea Finding** – "What ideas do I/we have?"
5. **Solution Finding** – evaluate the ideas and decide on the best solution.
6. **Acceptance Finding** – implement the best solution.

LATERAL THINKING

Lateral thinking is a method of thinking and solving problems in indirect and creative ways that aren't immediately obvious, or are 'outside of the box', so-to-speak. Where logic fails, lateral thinking can often save the day. It was pioneered, along with a handful of other creative thinking methodologies, by psychologist and author Edward de Bono, and involves the following:

- Relaxing rigid control of thinking
- Recognising the key aspects of the problem or situation as it's being perceived
- Searching for different ways of looking at the problem or situation

- Using chance to encourage other ideas (for example exploring possibilities – however unlikely)

Techniques involved might include:

- Free association (where those involved freely share thoughts, words, and anything else that comes to mind in association with the problem)
- Reversal (for example, when seeking to improve something, try first thinking about how you could make it much worse, then reverse those things)
- Distortion (look at the things you take for granted to be true and ask, "What if the opposite is true?"). Someone presumably once asked: "What if the earth isn't at the centre of our universe? What if the sun is at the centre, and the earth moves around it?"
- Literalisation (taking figurative language at face value – i.e. designing a clock that 'tells' – i.e. speaks the time.
- Fractionation (analysing a situation to determine the elements or components that it's made up of).

An example of lateral thinking would be where Granny is sitting in a chair knitting, and getting cross, because three-year-old Emily is playing with the wool. Parent 1 suggests putting Emily in the playpen. This would work but Emily's likely to get upset. Parent 2 suggests it might be a better idea to put Granny in the playpen to separate her (and the wool) from Emily.

CREATIVE THINKING

Creative thinking takes place in a different part of the brain than logical thinking does. You can stimulate it by trying some of the following activities:

- Listening to, or playing, some music
- Going for a walk
- Doing some other kind of physical exercise
- Doing some drawing, painting, photography
- Lying back and doing nothing for a while
- Meditating
- Brainstorming ideas with others – (maybe thinking up wacky purposes for everyday items)
- Using mind-maps and imagery.

It can also be helpful to pose a question to your subconscious mind before going to bed, asking it to come up with some answers, solutions or thoughts for you by the morning. You could also try posing a question to yourself on waking up, and then simply get in the shower and go about your business as usual, waiting for the solution to pop in when it's ready. It's often when our minds are relaxed that answers will come through, such as when we're driving along a familiar route and not having to think too much about it.

FORCE-FIELD ANALYSIS

This technique examines the forces influencing a situation - often a proposed change of some kind.

1. A facilitator writes a short description of the proposed change or problem in the centre of the page, where everyone can see it

2. They then ask the group to name the forces that are likely to help or hinder the change or problem

3. The facilitator then writes down each force, either to the left of the change or problem (usually the helpful, driving forces), or to the right (usually the restraining, hindering forces)

4. After the group has exhausted the list of forces, the facilitator leads a discussion with the aim of finding solutions that will strengthen the helpful forces, and remove or minimise the effect of the hindering forces.

SWOT ANALYSIS

This popular technique is often used as part of business planning, but can also be used by individuals on themselves. It is where you consider current **S**trengths and **W**eaknesses, along with any potential upcoming **O**pportunities and **T**hreats. It's often presented as a quadrant like the one to follow, where you list relevant things in the respective boxes:

	Helpful	Harmful
Internal	STRENGTHS	WEAKNESSES
External	OPPORTUNITIES	THREATS

Why not have a go at completing this one now, looking at the coming year? Once identified, you can create an action plan containing things you'll do to optimise your strengths and any opportunities, and manage your weaknesses and any threats.

You might find that drawing on your strengths could help minimise some of the threats, and that taking opportunities could help improve your weaknesses!

SIX THINKING HATS

Another tool from Edward de Bono, this one encourages broad thinking across all major thinking styles, aiming to make users more productive, focused, and involved (when thinking as a group), and enabling them to adopt a variety of perspectives, including those they ordinarily might not explore. It can be used by groups or individuals, and is especially useful in decision-making.

The process separates thinking into six styles or roles – each identified with a specific coloured hat. Users mentally imagine themselves wearing and switching the hats whilst exploring a topic, with each hat-change helping to focus or redirect their thoughts, until they have viewed things from all 6 perspectives. The hats represent the following:

- White – facts
- Red – feelings
- Yellow – benefits
- Black – cautions
- Green – ideas/creativity
- Blue – process.

CHAPTER 5 SUMMARY

✓ Much of the time, our thinking is happening outside of our conscious awareness. This is like driving on autopilot rather than in manual mode. Whilst that's not always a problem, there are times when it's more helpful to 'switch to manual', so that we're not only conscious of our thinking, but can also choose the thoughts we wish to think. Think of it as taking hold of the ship's steering wheel. Our thoughts create our experiences, so ensuring they are constructive and focused on what we want is much more likely to bring about positive outcomes.

✓ 'Right' thinking is the only kind of thinking that can bring about 'right' results. It's impossible to create positive outcomes whilst thinking negative thoughts. The thought is the cause – the outcome is the effect. Right thinking, which centres around thoughts of non-attachment, love, compassion, non-violence and helpfulness, can create miraculous results.

✓ Glorious thinking creates a glorious life. Hold in mind the most glorious visions of what you want to experience, and you can bring those visions to life. Glorious thoughts generate wonderful, high vibrational feelings that inspire positive actions, that bring about glorious outcomes. Create a daily practice of generating high-vibrational feelings such as love, joy, peace and gratitude, and work to maintain these feelings throughout the day.

✓ To become more courageous, confident and to feel good about ourselves, we need to consciously think thoughts of courage, confidence and self-esteem. Tell yourself you're a confident, courageous person (look for the evidence of this in your life – it is there!). You are also a decent and capable person, and could choose to feel good about yourself on that basis alone. You only need to change your thinking to experience these good feelings.

✓ Don't focus on problems. Instead, focus on solutions, and you'll be much more likely to find them. Know that there's a solution or way forward for every problem. Trust that all challenges will be overcome, and hold on to the mantra, "This situation is quickly and easily resolved for the highest good of all concerned."

✓ We tend to get what we focus on. 'Appreciative Inquiry' enables us to search for the best in people and situations, in order to accentuate and maximise the positives. What we appreciate, blossoms and grows.

✓ Questions are the answer, and the answers are always within. Whenever we feel stuck or don't know what to do, asking ourselves a great question can enable us to unlock thoughts and ideas that help us move forwards. The quality of the question will be reflected in the quality of the answer that comes forth. You may have to ask yourself more than one question.

✓ Thinking tools can be extremely helpful in facilitating effective thinking. Next time you're struggling to think in helpful ways, revisit the section on thinking tools, and see if something there might provide a helpful process or framework.

"RIGHT NOW, SOMEONE FAR LESS QUALIFIED THAN YOU IS LIVING YOUR DREAMS - ALL BECAUSE THEY DIDN'T JUST TALK ABOUT IT - THEY TOOK ACTION"

- BRAD SUGARS -

Chapter 6

WE CAN BRING OUR GOALS AND DREAMS TO LIFE

Albert Einstein reportedly said: "Imagination is everything. It is the preview of life's upcoming attractions," and it's true – the things we think about and visualise most often frequently show up in our lives in one form or another – eventually.

So often we think and speak in terms of what we don't want rather than what we want. The baked beans story illustrates this nicely...

A mother was preparing a meal for her young son. She emptied a tin of beans into a saucepan and put them on the stove to cook. Just then the phone rang - she was expecting a call, and wanted to take it. Mindful that she'd be leaving her little boy unsupervised for a minute or two, and wanting to prevent him from doing anything daft while she was out of the room, she firmly told him, "Stay here while I answer the phone. I'll be back soon; don't misbehave, and whatever you do, don't go putting those beans up your nose".

We're left to guess the outcome of this story!

Our words transfer mental images into the minds of those we're speaking with, so (perhaps especially with young children, who may be more inclined to blindly act on what they see and hear), we need to paint pictures of positive outcomes, or at least stop planting the seeds of unwanted disaster.

The story encourages us to think about times when we might have increased the likelihood of something we didn't want, just by thinking about it and highlighting the potential for it to happen. Can you think of a time when you imagined a situation that you didn't want to happen, and thought (or spoke) about it quite a lot until one day it did happen? Far better to use your imagination to envision situations that you do want to happen.

We have all the resources that we need within us to create the kind of lives that we want, and achieve the goals that we set ourselves. I believe we can pretty much have, do and be anything we like if we're determined, have faith and take consistent action; yet many of us don't seem to realise that, or perhaps don't really know what it is that we want.

Sometimes we allow ourselves to be talked out of our dreams and ambitions by well-meaning others who encourage us to 'be realistic'. Whilst there is of course a place for realism, it can often just be pessimism dressed up, and there may well be a way of achieving what we want if we look for it – especially if others not unlike us have achieved similar things before.

Sometimes we follow our dreams for a while, but then give up too soon when it doesn't appear to be happening, rather than rethink our strategy and change something we're doing. As

Winston Churchill is quoted as saying, "Success is the ability to move from one failure to another without loss of enthusiasm!"

Sometimes, we bumble through life with few or even no real aims or aspirations, simply reacting to what shows up and accepting what can often be an uninspired kind of existence; and maybe that's ok, if we're content with it. Our lives are, after all, ours to fill as we choose, and contentment is a positive emotion to live with. Certainly, grasping and striving too hard in the pursuit of material and achievement goals can be exhausting, and is ultimately unfulfilling when we get there and realise that the pleasure can be very short-lived before we begin craving the next thing.

It seems, though, that to some extent, we are goal-seeking missiles. Psychologist Abraham Maslow identified five key levels of human need, including biological/physiological needs; safety needs; belongingness and love needs; esteem needs; and self-actualisation needs (the latter being our need for to fulfil our potential and become all that we can be).

Our needs to survive, belong, give and receive love, to feel important, and for personal growth in order to fulfil our potential, drive pretty much all of our actions. It's like we're hard-wired to grow and evolve, and have an in-built need for progress. If we stand still for too long, and certainly when we stop learning (or at least when our learning considerably slows down), we may well get that itchy/antsy feeling and start to think about what's next.

I think most of us aspire to be happy, to do well and to be successful on some level – we just don't always have a clear vision of what that might mean doing. Again, that's probably ok.

We don't have to be able to see the bigger picture to find a few small goals that will keep us growing and progressing. We have a choice about whether to live a reactive kind of life, giving little or no thought to what we really want and simply responding to what shows up, or whether to choose a more pro-active kind of life where we establish some kind of vision, dream and/or goals, and then consciously take steps towards making these happen. There's no right or wrong in this – it's just choice and personal preference. Whilst we can't control outside events, we can control our thoughts and actions, and these are powerful, creative forces in our lives.

It's possible to literally design and build a life we will love, but so many of us prefer low expectations in a bid not to be disappointed! Not that life will ever really feel perfect. There will probably always be problems and challenges to overcome, and there's a danger that we can totally forget to enjoy ourselves and appreciate what we've got now, whilst we're working towards all the things that we want in the future. But life can, and arguably should, be largely good and rewarding, and we are the only ones that can make that happen.

WHAT DO YOU WANT, WHY, AND ARE YOU SURE?!

Making our goals, dreams and visions come to life first requires us to know (and be able to visualise) specifically what we want. Whilst we might not know exactly everything that we want, and in what sequence, we will probably have a few ideas. For example, one of my sons has no clue about what he wants to do with his life, but he does know that one day he'd like to build his own home and have a family and a husky. It's a start!

What this tells him is that he will either need to find work that enables him to earn a sufficient level of income to commission the building of a home to his specification, or that he'll need to learn some skills that will enable him to design and build a home himself. It might take him a while to build up to this level of skill or savings, but that's OK – he has time, and he understands that anything worthwhile doesn't usually happen overnight. At some stage, he'll also need to find himself a partner who'd like to have children, and then find someone who breeds huskies (or is selling one). Simple! Goals achieved.

Once we've decided what we want, it's a really good idea to consider why we want those things, and then check that we're sure they'll bring us the benefits we're looking for. One way of doing this is to ponder the following questions:

- Why do I want these things specifically? What are the benefits I think they will bring?
- Am I sure they will bring me the happiness I want?
- Do I understand what it will cost me (not just financially) to get them?
- Is it worth it, and am I prepared to pay the price?
- Is there another/easier/better way to achieve the benefits I'm looking for?

There's a saying that everything we want is because we think we'll feel better in having it, and that all the money in the world is spent on feeling good (or at least on avoiding feeling bad). For example, we might buy a flashy car because it gives us a feeling of being successful and prosperous. We might wear the designer clothes because they make us feel classier or more special. We might work hard to pay our bills, not because it feels good, but in order to avoid the pain of debt, bankruptcy and being chased for money!

What we want isn't always want we really want – it's often just the vehicle that we believe will deliver the good feelings that we want. So, when we think we want a nice car, what we might really want is to feel as good as other people. When we think we want designer clothes, what we might really want is more self-esteem, or to feel more valuable. These things might not actually bring us what we really want. We could just choose to do some inner work on realising our value and feeling good enough, and it would save us a lot of time and effort.

There's nothing inherently wrong about wanting nice things, and it can be fun working towards the achievement of the things that we like. But it's foolish to expect things to bring us happiness in themselves (because they can't), and we should remember that we can't take them with us at the end of our lives. Surely, life is about having some fun, finding some joy, learning and growing and maybe doing our bit for the greater good?! It shouldn't be about using money we've borrowed to buy things we don't need to impress people we don't like (to borrow from Robert Quillen's famous quote). We would be crazy to stress ourselves out chasing something that ultimately makes us unhappy.

Many of us spend our lives chasing transitory pleasures rather than working towards genuine, lasting happiness, but pleasure is generally short-lived and can quickly lead to feeling empty and craving more.

Things can only bring us happiness in as much as our thoughts about them will allow (remember, only thoughts cause feelings – things can't do that in themselves), and a lot of things are a bit empty in their promises. No point working hard all your life to achieve some big thing, only to find that once you've achieved it, it didn't deliver the benefits you'd anticipated.

Have you heard the story of the fisherman and the businessman?

A businessman was sitting by the beach in a small Brazilian village. As he sat, he saw a local fisherman rowing a small boat towards the shore, having caught quite few big fish. The businessman was impressed, and asked the fisherman, "How long does it take you to catch so many fish?". The fisherman replied, "Oh, just a short while." "Then why don't you stay longer at sea and catch even more?" asked the astonished businessman. "This is enough to feed my whole family," the fisherman said.

The businessman then asked, "So, what do you do for the rest of the day?" The fisherman replied, "Well, I usually wake up early in the morning, go out to sea and catch a few fish, then go back and play with my kids. In the afternoon, I take a nap with my wife and when evening comes, I join my buddies in the village for a drink — we play guitar, and sing and dance throughout the night."

The businessman offered a suggestion, "I am a PhD in business management. I could help you to become a more successful person. From now on, you should spend more time at sea and try to catch as many fish as possible. When you have saved enough money, you could buy a bigger boat and catch even more fish. Soon, you will be able to afford to buy more boats, set up your own company, your own production plant for canned foods and a distribution network. By then, you will have moved out of this village and to

Sao Paulo, where you can set up an HQ to manage your other branches."

The fisherman enquired, "And after that?" The businessman laughed heartily, "After that, you can live like a king in your own house and when the time is right you can go public and float your shares in the Stock Exchange and you will be rich." The fisherman asked, "And after that?"

The businessman replied, "After that, you can finally retire, you can move to a house by the fishing village, wake up early in the morning, catch a few fish then return home to play with kids, have a nice afternoon nap with your wife and when evening comes, you can join your buddies for a drink, play the guitar, sing and dance throughout the night!".

Psychologist Shawn Achor, in his book *The Happiness Advantage*, says that we've got it the wrong way around. We're taught that if we work hard, we'll be successful, and then we'll be happy. But it seems recent discoveries have shown that this formula is backwards - that happiness fuels success, and not the other way around. We could just choose to be happy regardless of what we have or haven't got, and the success may well come without us having to chase it.

This doesn't mean that we shouldn't set goals or work hard for what we want – just that it's well worth considering *why* we want it first of all, and being as sure as we can be that it will bring about the benefits we're hoping for.

For example, let's pretend (like my son) that you want to build your own home. Why exactly might that be? Is it so you can create a light, modern, airy space that meets your specific needs for comfort and utility, and where you'll feel happy and at home? What, specifically, would you need that you might not get in another kind of home, and why exactly do you want these things? What will it cost you to build your own home (think time, money, effort, difficulties, etc)? Will it be worth it, and are you prepared to pay the price? Are you sure it will bring you the happiness and benefits you're hoping for? Is there another/easier/better way to achieve those benefits?

This is not to talk ourselves or anyone else out of our dreams necessarily – it's just a safety check to ensure that what we think we want is the best way of getting what we really want. What we really want is usually a feeling. "I want a lovely home that feels light, airy and great to live in... where I'll feel happy and comfortable". There are probably easier options than self-building, although the easy option isn't necessarily the best one, and some would consider that it's still worth it.

I once attended a talk by Debra Corey of DebCo HR Ltd., where she spoke about her lifelong ambition to become the global head of reward within a large, multinational organisation. It took her many years and a heap of hard work to get there, but soon after achieving her goal, she realised it really wasn't what she wanted to do for the rest of her career. After stepping back and reassessing what was important to her, she changed track to focus on where she could make the biggest difference and achieve the most satisfaction, setting up her own company where she is now 'Chief Pay It Forward Officer'!

You can probably have or achieve anything you like, with a lot of hard work and effort – just make sure you think it all through first.

IT HELPS TO HAVE A DREAM

Once we're confident that what we want is likely to deliver what we really want, it helps to have a clear vision or dream. It's like we need to be able to see (and focus on) something with our inner vision, before things can begin happening in the outer world. As Stephen Covey said, the mental creation precedes the physical creation.

There's a saying that we are the writers, directors, producers and stars in our own lives; and there are similar sayings that suggest we are the artists that paint the masterpieces, or the sculptors that mould the clay of our lives. All good, creative imagery suggesting that we have free will to design and build our own lives and determine our own fates. What we probably won't ever know for sure is whether, and to what extent, there is input and co-creation from a higher power. My instinct is that it's largely free will, and that we can pretty much do and create what we want, but that we come into life with a pre-determined and often unconscious purpose and set of aptitudes that lead us in a particular direction. However, I also have a sense that we can call on a higher power to help and guide us when we need it, and that the help and guidance will always be forthcoming.

I don't know exactly what that higher power might be, and am not sure that anyone on earth can truly know the answer to this question. I can only encourage you check in with your intuition and believe what feels right to you. I do suspect, though, that when the chips are down and it feels like the end is coming, most people start praying to something or someone!

To begin designing the kind of life we'd love then, we need to work on developing a clear inner vision of what that life would look like. As the song goes, "You've got to have a dream. If you don't have a dream, how you gonna have a dream come true?"

The more detailed and compelling our vision is, and the more firmly and consistently we hold it in our minds, the stronger the driving force within us will be to bring it to life. The frequency and intensity with which we do this can make all the difference. But (and it's quite a big but!), we must really want to achieve our goal or vision. It would be hard to make something happen that we weren't that bothered about, so a good dose of passion and/or hunger is probably necessary.

It can be helpful to create a physical visual representation of what we want too, and vision boards (sometimes called dream boards) are a brilliant way of doing this. Whilst you could create an online vision board on Pinterest, Canva, Dream It Alive, and other similar sites (or even just draw or paint a picture), it's arguably more fun and more powerful to create a physical board that you can stick up on a wall somewhere in your home or workspace. Then, if you can spend seven minutes or so every day looking at the images and imagining (and feeling) that you've achieved those things, you'll be giving yourself the best possible chance of making them happen.

Of course, making it happen will also rely on taking action, so make sure you identify all the actions you can take that will begin to bring it all to life. As author and speaker Greg S. Reid says: "A dream written down with a date becomes a goal. A goal broken down into steps becomes a plan. A plan backed by action makes your dreams come true."

To create a vision board, you need a large piece of cardboard, a good stock of images, some scissors and paper glue. You can embellish your boards with felt pens, glitter, stickers, and so on, if wanted. Magazines, flyers, circulars and newspapers are all good image sources, or if you have a quality colour printer, you could simply print off images that you find online. Once you've sourced the words and images that match what you want, cut them out, then arrange them (dry at first) on your flat piece of cardboard and then when you're happy with the placement of your images, start sticking them down with glue. Finally, place your vision board somewhere you'll see it and be able to focus on it daily.

MANIFESTATION PROCESS

Bringing our goals, dreams and visions to life is a fairly straight-forward process that looks something like this:

Say it > See it > Believe it > Feel it > Act on it > Get it

Whilst actions don't always follow the exact, linear path that process models do, these are the steps that enable us to bring our goals to life. You'll probably have been doing most of them all your life anyway without consciously following a process. Here's a bit more detail on each of the steps:

Say it means that we voice our goals out load (it's also good to write them down on paper).

See it means that we clearly visualise the thing(s) we want.

Believe it means that we believe we'll make it happen (even if we're not sure how we'll do it yet).

Feel it means evoking all the amazing feelings we'll get when we achieve it.

Act on it means that we'll take the necessary/inspired action, adjusting our actions as needed.

Get it means that, having done all the above, we should eventually achieve our goal.

A large part of our success will depend on the specific actions we take towards our goal, and we may need to try several different things until we hit on the successful formula. There's likely to be some trial and error as we work it all out, and it will often take more than one course of action (and typically a combination of different things) to get us there in the end. If we pay attention to what's working and not working, and adjust our sails accordingly, we will usually get there in the end if we're determined.

If we've exhausted all avenues and something still isn't happening, it could be that we're subconsciously resisting what we want. For example, at a deeper level, we might be afraid to succeed, or we might not believe we're good enough, or feel we don't really deserve it for some reason. These things can potentially block us, so it's worth reflecting on whether any of these, or perhaps something similar, applies to us, and then working to challenge and change those fears and beliefs, or potentially working with a coach or therapist to help overcome them.

We can often make good progress by doing a bit of inner work on ourselves in visualisation and with self-talk. We just need to recognise that most of our fears aren't real – they're just thoughts that we have - often based on other people's lies and projections.

Another reason that something might not be happening for us could be to do with the goal itself, and our WHYs for wanting it. I believe that sound goals that are in our best interests and cause no detriment to others are easier to manifest. We might not always know what's ultimately in our own best interests (for example, there may be a higher purpose for our life that we haven't yet realised), hence, when stating and writing down our goals, we're encouraged to add the words "... or something even better..." to allow for this possibility.

Here are a few final reasons why something might not be happening for us:

- The goal is too big for us to believe we can do it (whilst it's good to dream big, it can help to break our goals down into more manageable, incremental steps)
- The goal isn't specific enough, or is too specific (it helps to have a clear vision of the kind of thing we want - the qualities, aspects and benefits - without restricting ourselves to one person, company, street, etc.)
- We're trying too hard (when we truly believe it will happen for us, we don't need to force it to happen)
- The time isn't quite right for us (this is about trusting that the universe knows best, and surrendering to divine timing!)

- We've got a bit more personal development to do before it can happen for us (it's helpful to identify the skills, qualities, etc. that we're not yet demonstrating, but will need in order to achieve our goal)
- We're not in alignment with what we want (i.e. we're not a vibrational match for our goal – maybe we need to relax more; or get happier; become more confident, and so on)
- Our goal is about someone else rather than ourselves (if this breaches a person's free will, it's likely to either not work, or to backfire).

THE R.A.S.

There's a part of our brain called the Reticular Activating System (or RAS) that filters out unnecessary information from the world around us and draws our attention to the 'important' stuff that we might otherwise miss amongst everything else. It knows what's 'important' to us from the kind of information we've recently or previously focused, on or given our attention to, a bit like how mobile phones and internet browsers remember our past searches, and then suggest content (usually adverts!) that we may be interested in.

We can consciously programme our RAS by focusing our attention often and intensely on the things, goals, dreams, etc. that we'd like to bring about, whilst saying what we want out loud as if it had already happened. This is like reprogramming the deeper part of ourselves with a set of instructions, which it will seek to make happen, (for example: "I'm so thrilled to have achieved a first-class honours degree, and found such a brilliant job"). Our RAS will then seek out, and draw our attention to, the opportunities, people and things that will help us to achieve our goals.

CHAPTER 6 SUMMARY

✓ With our thoughts and actions, we can bring our goals and dreams to life. Many of us manifest unconsciously and reactively, but we can become much more conscious, intentional and pro-active with it in order to create what we want.

✓ Creating a life we love starts with having a dream or a vision. We must know what we want first, or at least decide on something that would be fun to work towards, and that we would enjoy. Then we need to visualise this clearly and often, with as much feeling as we can muster.

✓ When we've worked out what we want, it's important to reflect on why we want it (i.e. the real reason, which is connected to feeling good or at least not feeling bad) and then check we're sure that it will deliver the benefits we want. We should avoid putting pressure on ourselves to chase money, titles and things that will bring us stress rather than happiness.

✓ To make something happen we need to <u>Say it</u> > <u>See it</u> > <u>Believe it</u> > <u>Feel it</u> > <u>Do it</u> > <u>Get it</u>. We may need to tweak our actions (the 'Do it' bit) and course-correct a few times, but if it's a worthy goal and we're determined, the chances are good that we'll get there in the end.

✓ We can programme our Reticular Activating System (RAS) to draw our attention to the information, opportunities and people that will be helpful to us in achieving our goals, by visualising and affirming what we wish to bring about, frequently and intensely.

"THERE IS NOTHING MORE IMPORTANT THAN DEVELOPING YOUR IMAGINATION TO TRANSFORM YOUR LIFE FROM THE INSIDE WORLD OF YOUR THOUGHTS AND FEELINGS, TO THE OUTSIDE WORLD OF YOUR RESULTS AND MANIFESTATIONS"

- NEVILLE GODDARD -

Chapter 7

WE CAN TRANSFORM ANY RESULT

Cast your mind back to the 'Coaching Wheel' activity in Chapter 1, where you considered your satisfaction scores across the various aspects of your life.

It's very possible to transform these scores (and more specifically, the results you're getting in these areas) by following a simple process that reverses the T-F-A-R model also covered in Chapter 1 (Thoughts > Feelings > Actions > Results).

The reason you're getting these results is largely based on your actions, behaviours, choices and decisions; however, these are being driven by your thoughts and feelings, which in turn are being influenced by the situation you find yourself in.

THE R-A-F-T MODEL

When we reverse the T-F-A-R process, it becomes possible to create change, and transform anything. So, we need to work backwards from the results we're getting to the thoughts that first initiated them.

Introducing the R-A-F-T model:

> **Results < Actions < Feelings < Thoughts**

With R-A-F-T, we first consider the results we want to achieve, then work out the specific actions it will take to deliver those results. Then, we identify the kinds of feelings and thoughts we'll need to support these actions. Finally, we pinpoint some strategies that will enable us to think, feel and do what's necessary, before considering what might get in the way, and implementing some strategies for overcoming these things.

This sounds quite simple, and technically it is, except for the fact that it can take some time and experimentation to pinpoint the specific actions it will take to bring about the results we want, and also because it's not always as easy as we might think to change our behaviour patterns and thinking. There's an element of inside-out transformation required here rather than a quick fix, although it doesn't have to involve a lot of time or pain to achieve it.

Transformation means a marked change in form, nature or appearance. Whilst it's relatively straight-forward to change something on the level of appearance, true and lasting transformation takes place on the inside. This is why the milkshake diets we can buy in the pharmacies and supermarkets don't tend to result in sustainable or permanent weight loss, because they don't retrain our eating habits, and do nothing to help us understand and overcome the physical, mental and emotional factors that cause us to overeat. As an aside, they're also full of sugar – a highly addictive substance, and key contributor to obesity. If we can stick to the shakes, we can lose weight quickly and dramatically. However, without long-term dependency on them, the weight tends to pile back on again as quickly as it came off.

The 'Inside-Out' understanding of the nature of human experience, which describes how our outer experiences are created by what's going on inside of us, has gained momentum in recent years and is almost becoming a mainstream idea. 'Supercoach' Michael Neill has possibly had the greatest impact in bringing this understanding to the public arena in recent years, and has made popular the principle that our experience comes from our thinking.

Whilst this might not be a comfortable realisation (it means that we, and not other people, are responsible for everything we are feeling), it does mean that we can begin to change our experience just by recognising and moving beyond the thoughts that are causing it. The saying "Don't believe everything you think" springs to mind. Whatever emotion we're feeling is coming from our thinking rather than from the situation (or person) itself. Yes, they can provide us with a strong invitation to feel a certain way, for sure, but we don't necessarily have to feel bad, mad, sad, or any other feeling as a response, if we choose not to. The trick is to centre ourselves, breathe, stay calm and get solution-focused.

So – our experience of life is an inside job, and the results we get reflect what's going on inside of us. If we want to change our lives, our experiences and/or the results that we're getting, we need to change what's happening on the inside of us (how we think, how we feel and what we do). Only then can we be sure to achieve lasting transformation.

So... are you ready for some personal transformation? Then read on!

THE SUNSHINE METHOD

The model below outlines my process for changing any result. I call it 'The Sunshine Method', after my training consultancy business, 'Sunshine Corporate & Personal Development', because this is the process I follow when helping people and organisations to achieve their goals and transform their results.

Before starting, I invite clients to consider what will happen if they don't take any steps to improve the situation they want to change. The answer is usually either that nothing will change or that things will get worse (a bit like with household maintenance, doing nothing usually results in further decline). I then invite them to fully explore what the negative consequences of that could be (our imaginations are usually very good at picturing this!) and ask them if they wish to avoid this pain. I also ask what the amazing benefits of making changes would be (aside from just getting a better result) – particularly in relation to the people and things they value. This helps to connect clients with their inner motivation for change, and knowing/recalling these things helps to keep them going when the going gets tough.

THE 'SUNSHINE' METHOD

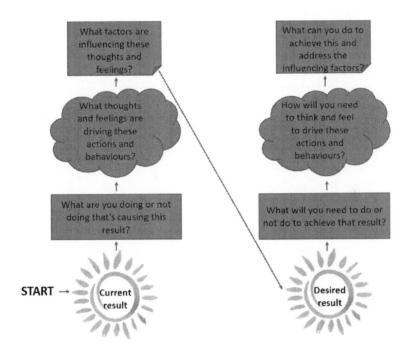

I use an almost identical process when working to achieve change with organisations, which refers to 'your people' rather than 'you', although I like to work one-to-one with the individual leaders and managers too, using the version above to focus on their own input. I find that what the managers and leaders in an organisation do and don't do (and how they do and don't do it) always has a powerful impact on how those around them think, feel and act/behave. In fact, some trainers and consultants no longer work with team members directly when approached to do training at that level, insisting that they work with the management teams instead.

To explain the method:

- You start by defining the current result you're getting that you'd like to change. It's good to state this as a measurement – for example (taking the Wheel of Life activity from Chapter 1):

"My satisfaction score for Health & Fitness is only 5"; or "I'm fat and unfit – I am breathless after jogging for 30 seconds and I weigh 14½ stones"; or "My size Large clothes are far too tight".

- You consider what it is that you're doing and/or not doing that's bringing about this result (i.e. you think about your actions, habits, behaviours and the choices and decisions you're making).

"I don't take any formal exercise. I eat and drink what I want, when I want it, in generous portions. I snack in the evenings after my dinner, and when I feel tired, stressed or down. I don't plan meals and end up eating a lot of take-aways. I have a daily (sometimes twice daily) chai latte habit, and eat sweets and/or chocolate every day. I generally avoid getting on the scales."

- You reflect on the feelings that have been driving these actions and behaviours.

"I feel fat and unattractive. I have little energy or motivation for exercise, and feel tired a lot of the time. I don't really know what to do with the difficult, uncomfortable feelings that I get, and food helps me to relax and forget everything. It's my way of treating myself."

- You ponder the thoughts, beliefs, attitudes, opinions, etc. that are likely to be creating these feelings.

  "I'm just a fat, ugly person. We're all big in my family – it's in the genes. It's so hard to lose weight – you must starve yourself just to lose a measly pound or two a week. Exercise is boring... all that effort just to burn off a few hundred calories. Junk food tastes good, and healthy food tastes like cardboard. Also, I can't cook. I would rather be fat and happy than miserable and thin. I deserve to have some pleasure in life. What would I do without my snacks? How would I fill my time? How would I cheer myself up and manage my emotions?"

- You identify what might be happening around you that's not helping you (i.e. situations that are influencing what and how you're thinking, feeling and doing, or otherwise reinforcing the result you're getting).

  "My housemate loves to eat, and we can be a bad influence on each other. There are five different fast food outlets at the top of our road. The supermarkets always have cheap and irresistible offers on bags of donuts, cookies and multipacks of crisps and chocolate. Every time I go to my parents' house, they feed me up. My job is super-stressful - I come home so tired and drained, all I want to do is lie down and eat. My boss is always putting me down. I have no partner to want to look good for."

- Then you think about the result you want instead. You check that it's reasonable and achievable, and that you're prepared to work for it and/or maybe experience a bit of discomfort to achieve it.

"I would like to have a Health & Fitness score of 8 / be able to jog for 20 minutes without wanting to collapse / weigh 11 stones / fit comfortably into size Medium clothes."

- You consider what you'll need to do, and maybe not do, to bring about this result (looking at the actions, habits, behaviours, and the choices and decisions you'll need to be making).

"I'd need to eat smaller and better meals. I'd need to stop snacking so much – especially sweets and chocolate in the evenings. Start cooking meals from scratch with fresh ingredients – maybe sign up for a cookery class. Stop getting take-aways or only get one occasionally. Swap my chai latte for a specialty tea or standard Americano. Take at least 5,000 steps every day (and ideally 10,000). Sign up to an exercise or gym class that I'll enjoy – maybe get my housemate to come too. Find something else to do when I'm feeling down, like a creative hobby, going for a walk or jog, calling a friend... maybe writing everything down in a journal, or taking a relaxation or meditation course. I will also keep my thoughts positive and constructive, and do what I can every day to feel good, like enjoying the sunshine, listening to uplifting music, and so on."

- You reflect on the feelings you'll need to be experiencing to drive these actions and behaviours.

"I'll need to feel good more of the time. It would help to feel

less tired. I'll need to value myself a bit more, and want to nourish myself and look good for myself and no-one else. To feel strong and able to cope with difficult, uncomfortable feelings – allowing myself to listen to them and work out what actions I need to take."

- You identify the thoughts, beliefs, attitudes, opinions, etc. you'll need to hold to create these feelings.

"Losing weight is almost easy for me. I really enjoy eating healthy food that I've cooked myself from scratch. Healthy food tastes delicious and it also gives me energy. Junk food makes me feel sluggish and horrible. I deserve to look good and feel great. I do exercise that I enjoy and it feels amazing. I'm in the process of transformation. I am looking forward to watching my body change and flourish. I'm looking forward to buying some great new clothes that I'll feel amazing in."

- Finally, you consider what you can do about the things happening around you that aren't helping you, so it becomes easier for you to do what you need to do.

"I can talk to my boss about my workload, and the way he/she speaks to me. I could even consider changing my job for something less stressful and where I'd feel more valued. I could speak to my housemate and parents about my goal, and ask for their support in not encouraging me to overeat. I could avoid walking to the top of our road where all the fast-food outlets are. I could shop at the street market instead of the supermarket, so I'm not tempted by all the junk-food offers (and shop when I'm not hungry). I could

even look for a partner who enjoys healthy living."

This is just one example of the steps you might follow when using the Sunshine Method to tackle a result you'd like to change. It's over to you now. Look at the scores from your 'Wheel of Life' activity (Chapter 1) and consider the lowest scoring/highest priority area that you'd like to see improvements in, and have a go at completing the following:

Firstly, consider your WHYs... the reasons why it's important for you to make changes now. Write down several reasons if possible – maybe two that link with your hopes, i.e. the benefits you want, and two that link with your fears, i.e. the negative consequences you don't want. Make them as emotive (and therefore powerful) as you can, as this will help to keep you motivated throughout.

_____

_____

_____

_____

_____

_____

_____

_____

_____

_____

_____

Review these often – especially if you're finding it difficult to stick to the actions (and thoughts/feelings) that will deliver the desired result. Once you've finished, have considered your WHYs and are feeling sufficiently motivated to act, you're ready to begin the process:

Define the current result you're getting that you'd like to change (in measurable terms)

_____

_____

_____

_____

_____

_____

What are you doing and/or not doing that's bringing about this result (i.e. your actions, habits, behaviours and the choices and decisions you're making)?

_____

_____

_____

_____

_____

_____

What feelings have been driving these actions and behaviours?

_____

_____

_____

_____

_____

_____

_____

_____

What thoughts, beliefs, attitudes, opinions, etc. are creating these feelings?

_____

_____

_____

_____

_____

_____

_____

_____

_____

What's happening around you that might be influencing you to think/feel/do what you're doing, or otherwise reinforcing the result you're getting?

_____

_____

_____

_____

_____

_____

_____

What result do you want instead? (Check this is reasonable and achievable and that you're prepared to work for it and/or experience a bit of discomfort to achieve it).

_____

_____

_____

_____

_____

_____

_____

_____

What will you need to do (and maybe not do) to bring about this result (consider your actions, habits, behaviours and the choices and decisions you'll be making)?

_____

_____

_____

_____

_____

_____

_____

_____

What feelings will you need to be experiencing to drive these actions and behaviours?

_____

_____

_____

_____

_____

_____

_____

_____

_____

What kind of thoughts, beliefs, attitudes, opinions, etc. will you need to hold to create these feelings?

_____

_____

_____

_____

_____

_____

_____

_____

_____

What can you do about the things happening around you that aren't helping you, so it becomes easier for you to do what you need to?

_____

_____

_____

_____

_____

_____

_____

_____

To follow are some additional questions that will be helpful to ask yourself:

When will you start?

_____

_____

_____

_____

What will you need, and from whom?

_____

_____

_____

_____

_____

How will you hold yourself to account? (Can you ask a friend to check in with you periodically, for example, to see how you're getting on and provide a bit of support and challenge if you need it?)

_____

_____

_____

_____

_____

You may well find that following this process works first time for you, but it's possible that it might not. Sometimes, and particularly when the result you wish to change is more complex and/or will involve other people changing what they do (as is usually the case in corporate/organisational projects), there will be some tweaking that needs to be done along the way. For example, you might need to reconsider the actions you've focused on as being critical to success (you may have overlooked something important, or be focusing on actions that aren't that crucial to success), or to the strategies you've pinpointed for dealing with the stuff that gets in the way.

There are quite a lot of things that can influence how we think, how we feel and what we do. Whilst it's possible to achieve a level of mastery or transcendence where we're no longer affected by these things (or are perhaps less affected by them), this can take quite a long time (even a lifetime) to achieve, and some of us may never achieve it.

Whilst we're working towards mastery or transcendence, we will probably need some strategies for managing (or being less affected by) these influences, which can include:

- **the people around us, what they do, how they behave, what they encourage and discourage in us.** I'll never forget a grown man high-fiving one of my sons (who was about four at the time) in a hardware superstore, for belching very publicly and loudly. My son still thinks loud, public belching is heroic behaviour, despite our best attempts to teach him otherwise! We need to be able to manage our own (and deal with other people's) demeanour and moods, and may need to learn some new skills such as saying no to what we don't want, asserting some boundaries, and so on.

- **the systems, structures and processes we come into contact with.** These are things of human design that have usually been created with the intention of being helpful and improving or managing things, but which can sometimes have the effect of causing problems and/or being unhelpful. Examples include the legal system, government system, education system, healthcare system, welfare system, transport system, organisational structure, business structure, hierarchies, religions, families, networks, work patterns, business processes, policies and procedures, brand standards, manufacturing processes, triage processes, etc. We need to be able to navigate these, challenging and changing what we can (along with other people if necessary), and accepting or finding workarounds for the stuff that we can't influence.

- **the resources and things that we have (and don't have) at our disposal.** This can include the supplies, tools and equipment we have at our disposal, the facilities we can access, the money we have, the services available to us, and so on. We may need to become more creative about how we acquire the resources we need (and how we replace anything that's not helping us).

- **our environment.** This could be our home, our place of work, the village, town or city we live in, the general climate we experience, variances in weather, and so on. We need to make sure that our environment is working for us and not against us, and make changes where possible.

This could be as radical as moving (consider the saying "If you don't like where you are, move... you are not a tree!") or simply changing something about our environment or how we're experiencing it.

There is a saying in the field of change management that says, "Every system is perfectly designed to get the results that it's getting." In other words, your world is perfectly set up to get the results that you're currently getting, so if you want different results, you will probably need to change something in the outer world (as well as the inner world).

Don't be discouraged if you don't achieve the results you want immediately. It's all experimental in the beginning, and it's relatively easy to change your strategy. Keep going, keep tweaking and the chances are good that you'll get there in the end.

As mentioned earlier, the Sunshine Method can also be used to transform corporate/organisational results, and the version used for this is almost identical to the one used with individuals.

This version refers to 'people' rather than 'you', and the method would normally be worked through twice – once from the perspective of the leaders and managers, and once from the perspective of the non-managerial staff.

Have a read-through of the model:

THE 'SUNSHINE' METHOD - ORGANISATIONS

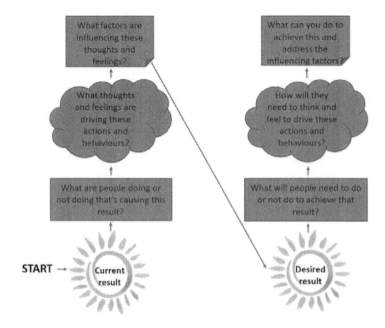

Here's an example:

- Define the current result you're getting that you'd like to change, in a way that can be measured and progress tracked.

   Currently, staff take an average of 9 days' sickness absence per annum.

- What are your people doing, and/or not doing, that's bringing about this result (i.e. the actions, habits, behaviours and the choices and decisions they're making)?

   Some may be taking on more work than they can cope with and working too hard and for too long. Some struggle to say no to certain requests, and people and aren't speaking up or asking for help when they need it.

Some aren't balancing their energy output with renewal activity, like not taking proper breaks or ensuring they balance work with leisure activities that refresh them.

Some staff members don't pro-actively look after themselves, eating badly, not getting enough sleep, not exercising, drinking too much, and so on.

They might not all be considering the potential risks and consequences of their leisure pursuits on their ability to do their jobs.

Managers are not all providing their staff with the environment and means to feel happy and engaged in their work. They don't all nurture their relationships with staff, or inspire a sense of loyalty, trust and teamwork.

Managers aren't all as knowledgeable as they could be regarding well-being. They're not all confident in how to support and manage unwell staff, and don't tend to ask many questions of employees regarding their symptoms and what may have triggered them. For example, some people call in sick for minor (and in some cases, lifestyle related) reasons. Maybe they didn't get a good night's sleep; or they have a tickly cough; or hay-fever; maybe they're hung-over; they're a bit sore after too much sun at the weekend; they have a headache, or stomach-ache, or sore throat, etc. (These things are situational, of course, and sometimes it would be appropriate to stay off with some of these symptoms – for example, depending on severity, and if there's an infection present or an accompanying fever. In mild cases the person might be able to take a remedy, come in to work and see how they get on).

- What feelings have been driving these actions and behaviours?

  (Some of this might be guess-work but you can interview or survey your people to find out exactly how they're feeling, what they're thinking, and what's influencing them. This is true of the next two questions also).

  Feeling fatigued and generally low in energy/enthusiasm.

  Experiencing a low level of engagement and enjoyment in their work.

  Feeling stressed and/or overwhelmed with the nature and/or volume of work.

  Feeling angry about how they perceive they're being treated.

  Not coping with changes that are being brought in.

  Feeling that work's not that important.

  Feeling entitled to take sick leave, whatever the symptoms/reasons.

- What thoughts, beliefs, attitudes, opinions, etc. are creating these feelings?

  Thinking that they aren't responsible for their well-being – that they can't help getting sick (there may be some validity in this in some instances).

Believing it's acceptable to call in sick for these reasons - other people do and it's seemingly not challenged.

Not thinking about the impact or pressure on the organisation, their manager or colleagues.

Believing that sick leave is an annual allowance they're entitled to on top of their holiday leave.

Generally thinking negatively, which weakens the immune system and makes them more vulnerable to illness.

Believing illness is a normal part of everyday life no matter what you do, and expecting to catch colds and/or 'flu' every year.

Not understanding the causes of illness, or knowing how they can be prevented.

- What's happening around your people that might be influencing them to think/feel/do these things or that's otherwise reinforcing the result you're getting?

  Workloads and management styles are triggering stress and resulting in disengagement in some areas.

  They see people around them going off sick all the time.

  There aren't that many good role-models around them pro-actively nurturing their own well-being.

  It's easy for people to call in sick, and there are few

drawbacks for doing so.

There are few benefits (and no medals!) for maintaining a good level of attendance.

Many don't have a strategy for dealing with stress, and haven't developed the skills of resilience, which may be making them more prone to becoming sick.

Environmental factors might be contributing. For example, the workplace is somewhat drab and dreary in appearance, and people speculate about the air conditioning spreading germs.

A lack of knowledge about well-being, the causes of stress and ill-health (and how to avoid them), what the body needs (and doesn't need) for maximum well-being, and so on.

There's a general low level of energy and motivation.

There's a lack of guidance (and no formal process) for managers to follow when sickness absence becomes frequent for an individual.

- What result do you want instead? (Check these are reasonable and achievable, and will be worth the hard work, disruption and discomfort it might take to achieve it).

  We want to see an average of no more than 5 days' sickness absence taken per person per annum.

- What will your people need to do (and maybe not do) to bring about this result? Consider the actions, habits, behaviours and choices/decisions they'll need to be making).

Staff members will need to be able to balance their energy output with energy renewal activity – i.e. working productively but not overworking, taking proper breaks, keeping a check on their work-life balance, etc.

Managers will need to encourage and monitor the above.

Staff members will need to be more pro-active in looking after their well-being - physically, mentally, emotionally and spiritually.

Staff members will need to know when and how to say no to relevant requests and people, and to ask for help when they need it.

Managers will need to encourage staff members to consider the potential risks and consequences of their leisure pursuits on their ability to do their jobs.

Managers will need to be able to manage well-being and sickness absence, including knowing the appropriate questions to ask, and at what stages.

Managers will also need to be confident and explorative when taking sick calls, regarding what's appropriate to ask and say at this stage and what should wait until the staff member returns to work.

Managers will need to nurture their relationships with staff members, inspire a sense of loyalty, trust and teamwork in them, and create an environment where staff members feel happy and engaged in their work.

- What feelings will they need to be experiencing to drive these actions and behaviours?

Staff members will need to feel:

Energetic, enthusiastic and engaged in their work, understanding the importance of their role and purpose.

Less stressed and/or overwhelmed.

More accepting and in control of the changes that are being brought in.

That sick leave is a privilege to be drawn on when genuinely needed, rather than an automatic right or allowance.

Managers will need to feel:

Confident in their abilities to support and manage staff.

Supported and well themselves.

- What kind of thoughts, beliefs, attitudes, opinions, etc. will they need to hold to create these feelings?

For staff members:

"My well-being is largely something that I can influence and take responsibility for."

"It's OK to take time off sick when I'm not well, or have something contagious. If I have a minor ailment, I will take a remedy and see how I get on."

"I have the skills to manage my time, deal with stress, adapt to change, and nurture my well-being. I am resilient."

"My manager cares about my physical, mental and emotional well-being. I'm encouraged to work productively, but also to take breaks, balance my energy and not burn out."

"If I have a problem of any kind, there's someone at work I can talk to, and they will help me work things out."

"I enjoy my work, and being part of this team and organisation. I am committed to our success."

For managers (in addition to the above):

"I have the skills, knowledge and support that I need to engage, support and manage my team through challenging times, nurturing my own and others' well-being, and creating a positive environment where we can all thrive."

- What can you do about the things happening around them and influencing them that aren't helping, so it becomes easier for them to do what they need to do?

Training for staff:

Well-being awareness (Inc. building resilience; coping with change; time management).

Training for managers:

Employee engagement; Managing well-being; Managing absence; Managing Change.

Write and communicate a procedure on 'Managing Sickness Absence'. Ensure managers follow the formal procedure if a member of staff takes more than 5 days/2 absences in a rolling 6-month period, in consultation with HR (and if the circumstances warrant it).

Write/communicate a "Taking Sickness Absence' procedure.

Re-paint drab areas of the building, improve the lighting and bring in some colourful fittings.

Have the air-conditioning unit deep-cleaned regularly.

Introduce some well-being activities such as lunchtime walks, after-work singing group, Monday morning mindfulness sessions, maybe a monthly visit from a masseur.

Do more to support people around change – consulting them as far as is practical, communicating often, and making the change as easy as possible for them.

Recognition for those that take no sickness absence in a year (the manager makes a point of having a face to face conversation with relevant individuals, thanking them for their reliability). Note, it is probably not a good idea to have a reward scheme for attendance incentives, as this could deter people from staying off when they're not fit to work, and could discriminate against those with protected conditions. Whilst being pro-active around our health should result in improved health and attendance, there is probably a bit of luck involved too.

Appoint a few Well-being Champions who role-model good habits and encourage others to look after themselves too.

When will you start?

_____

_____

_____

_____

_____

What will you need, and from whom?

_____

_____

_____

_____

_____

How will you track progress?

_____

_____

_____

_____

_____

Communicate your goal with your people, sharing your WHYs, your strategy (or at least the bits that are relevant to them), and make sure you clearly explain and emphasise what's in it for them. Always remember to celebrate successes and give credit where it's due.

TRANSFORMING YOURSELF

We've discussed how real, lasting transformation happens from the inside-out... from reviewing and re-setting our minds (our thoughts, pictures, beliefs, concepts and attitudes, etc). This changes how we feel, which inspires more constructive actions and behaviours. However, a bit of outside-in activity can powerfully change how we feel too, and shouldn't be dismissed or underestimated.

Here are some examples of outside-in transformation activities that can make us feel amazing:

- **Standing tall.** Imagine an invisible piece of string or rope going up through your spine and being pulled upwards from the top of your head.
- **Belly breathing.** Take conscious control of your breathing, filling your belly first, then your chest. This oxygenates your system, helping you to feel calmer and more confident.
- **Grounding ourselves.** Sense your connection with the ground under your feet. Imagine sending roots from your feet deep down into the earth.
- **Centring ourselves.** Take a deep breath in and bring your awareness to the present moment. Focus your mind on the area just below your belly button (bring your hand

there too if it helps) and continue to breathe and hold your awareness here.

- **Doing the superhero power pose!** Stand with your feet hip-width apart. Pull yourself up to your fullest height and place your hands on your hips with your shoulders back. This makes you feel instantly more confident.

- **Smiling.** Relax your facial muscles and bring a smile to your mouth and eyes. Consciously breathe and smile for at least a minute. Relax even more. Feel the good chemicals as they begin to flood your brain and body.

- **Exercising.** Find an exercise that you enjoy, and do it when you can. You could choose something like yoga if you want to feel calmer and more centred, or something like kickboxing if you want to feel stronger and more confident. You could just buy a skipping rope and grab five minutes to skip a few times throughout the day. In fact, you don't really need any equipment - just get down on the floor periodically and do some sit-ups or press-ups. You'll feel stronger mentally as well as physically, and get the bonus of endorphins flooding your system.

- **Grooming.** Taking care of your appearance (face, hair, nails, etc) can help you to feel more polished and together, which can influence your actions and behaviours. A bit of make-up can make a big difference (natural make-up ranges for men are even starting to pop up now too), and having well-styled hair could make you feel smarter and more capable. A study by Yale University revealed that when we feel confident about our hair, we feel confident in ourselves and our abilities, which can boost our happiness and professional success.

- **Dressing well.** What you wear can have a massive impact on how confident or relaxed you feel. According to Michael Slepian, author of The Cognitive Consequences of Formal Clothing, formal clothing makes us feel more powerful, authoritative and competent, and casual clothing makes us feel more relaxed and friendly. Wearing clothes that make us look and feel good helps us to approach life more confidently.

- **Wearing colour.** Colour has a significant effect on mood and performance, although the effect of different colours on different people varies. Researchers at the University of Essex found that, in general, brighter colours make us feel happier, as well as boosting our memory, mental agility, reaction times and strength. If you've never had a colour consultation to help you find the colours that work best for you (and the ones that don't), it's worth the investment, and you can get advice on the shapes and styles that suit your body type and personality too.

- **Investing in great underwear.** Whilst it's important to be able to breathe properly and feel comfortable, good undergarments that enhance your shape can not only improve your look – they can also make you feel more confident. Even if you don't need help smoothing or enhancing your shape, wearing underwear that looks good and is comfortable (it's possible to get both!) can make you feel great.

These are mostly surface-level things that, in themselves, are unlikely to create real and lasting transformation. If we only feel good after two hours spent in hair, make-up and wardrobe, for example, that could be a problem; but when we combine some of these outside-in activities with the inner work previously outlined in this book, we have a winning combination for maximising our confidence, and with that, our ability to achieve our goals.

FAKE IT 'TIL YOU MAKE IT?

A lot has been said about 'faking it until you make it', and whilst I wouldn't encourage anyone to be fake and pretend to be someone they're not, I think it's perfectly OK to start acting as if you already are the best, most confident version of yourself that you'd like to be.

When we act as if we already are the person we want to become, or as if we've already achieved our goals and dreams (and we believe that these things are already 'in the bag' for us just a little further down the road), we're far more likely to make them happen. Consider the following questions:

> **What would happen if you acted as if you were an amazing, confident person?**
>
> **What would happen if you acted as if almost anything was possible for you?**
>
> **What would happen if you acted as if you were already a success?**

What would happen if you acted as if your needs would always be met abundantly?

What would happen if you acted as if you had all the love and support you ever needed?

What would happen if you acted as if there was no such thing as failure?

What would happen if you acted as if you were utterly gorgeous?

What would happen if you acted as if you had everything you could ever need?

What would happen if I told you these things are all already true?

Ok – now it's your turn.

What would happen if you acted as if... (*insert goals or aspirations below*)?

_____

_____

_____

_____

_____

_____

_____

_____

_____

_____

_____

_____

_____

_____

_____

_____

Take a moment to picture and feel that now, as if it had already happened. Intensify these pictures and feelings. Do this every day, and never doubt the miraculous power of your mind to bring you what you think about. Your thoughts and feelings are so powerful, you can literally make this happen.

Your faith needs to be stronger than your fears and doubts, so if you catch unhelpful thoughts popping in (as they probably will from time to time), try and catch them early. Acknowledge them and then tell them to relax – that you've got this, and that all is well.

CHAPTER 7 SUMMARY

✓ To transform any result in any area of your life, remember R-A-F-T. To secure the Result you want, you'll need to consider the Actions, Feelings and Thoughts that will get you there.

✓ Use the Sunshine Method to work out the details. First, connect to your intrinsic motivation. Write down some emotive reasons why that result is important to you, that connect with your hopes (i.e. the benefits you want) and your fears (i.e. the negative consequences you don't want). These are your WHYs. Then, look at what you're doing, not doing, feeling and thinking that's creating the result you're currently getting, and what's happening around you that might be encouraging that, and/or not helping you. Then, work backwards from the result you want, pinpointing the specific actions that will be needed to achieve it, and then the feelings and thoughts you'll need to drive those actions. Make relevant changes where you can to the things happening around you that aren't helping you. Consider what and who can help you, and take the relevant action. Tweak as necessary. Review your WHYs frequently, especially if you find yourself struggling and wanting to give up.

✓ When seeking personal transformation, consider which of the outside-in confidence building activities listed in this chapter might strengthen, supplement and reinforce your efforts. Never underestimate the power of feeling and looking good in helping you achieve your goals.

✓ Start acting as if you're an amazing, confident person (note: this can be quiet confidence if extraversion feels uncomfortable); that almost anything is possible for you; that you are already a big success; that your needs will always be met abundantly; that you have all the love and support you'll ever need; that there's no such thing as failure; that you are utterly gorgeous; that you have everything you could ever need; and that all of these things are true. If you're struggling with any part of this, just use your imagination! Remember Albert Einstein's quote about imagination being the preview of life's coming attractions.

"WITH HEALTH, EVERYTHING IS A SOURCE OF PLEASURE; WITHOUT IT, NOTHING ELSE, WHATEVER IT MAY BE, IS ENJOYABLE. HEALTH IS BY FAR THE MOST IMPORTANT ELEMENT IN HUMAN HAPPINESS"

- ARTHUR SCHOPENHAUER-

Chapter 8

LOOKING AFTER OUR THINKING EQUIPMENT

If we don't eat well, sleep well, get enough fresh air and exercise; if we smoke, drink too much, or otherwise take in substances that aren't good for us; if we over-work, under-play or ignore our emotional needs, then we won't feel or function at anything like our best, and probably won't achieve and maintain the kinds of goals or results that we'd like to.

In order to think, feel and operate at our best (and thereby get the best outcomes and results), we need to look after ourselves in the holistic sense. This doesn't mean that we must be 100% virtuous all the time, or that life must be boring and devoid of any fun. It just means that we need to be a bit canny about balancing our wellbeing needs, and making sure that – for most of the time at least – we're doing what helps us, and not what harms us.

Our different aspects (physical, mental, emotional and spiritual) are all intertwined and interdependent, so it's not enough to focus only in terms of looking after our physical selves. We also need to consider the other three aspects – our mind, our emotions and our spirit:

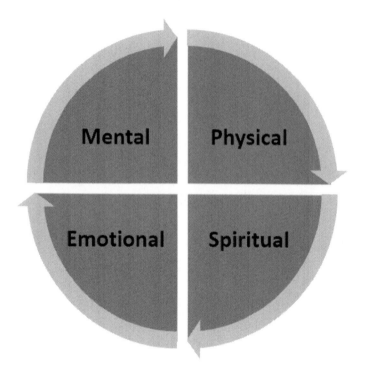

- PHYSICAL = our brain, heart, gut and body in general.
- MENTAL = our thinking mind.
- EMOTIONAL = the feelings that we experience.
- SPIRITUAL = our spirit, soul or life force

THE PHYSICAL ASPECT

The study of neuroscience has shown that there are three 'brains' (or centres of intelligence) in the body. They are in our head (our cephalic, or actual brain), our heart (our cardiac brain) and our gut (our enteric brain). We tend to make some decisions with our head (the kind that require a rational approach); some with our heart (the kind that require an emotional approach); and some with our gut (the kind that require an intuitive approach). When we're not sure what to do, it can be useful to consult all three in alignment.

To function at our best, it makes sense to look after these physical organs (and our bodies in general). Most of us know the basic principles of a healthy lifestyle for optimal physical well-being, but we don't always follow all them as closely as we could. Here's a reminder of some key well-being dos and don'ts:

Do...	Don't...
Eat a balanced diet (with sufficient protein, quality fats and complex carbohydrates), ideally in 3 meals a day consisting of natural, unprocessed foods.	Eat highly processed junk food or snack constantly. Similarly, don't skip meals or go too long between eating.
Drink plenty of clean, filtered water – around 8 glasses a day, or 2 litres as a very rough guide. Water boosts brain function (including concentration and working memory), energy and mood.	Eat the foods (or drink the drinks) known to trigger bad moods, including those containing refined sugars, dried fruits, refined cereals, grains high in gluten, bagels and many baked goods (such as cakes and cookies), processed meats, coated nuts, fried snack foods like crisps and chips, and hydrogenated and saturated fats.

Do...	Don't...
Keep active, exercising regularly and including aerobic, strength, balance and flexibility training.	Drink lots of fizzy drinks – diet varieties or otherwise.
Get a good night's sleep (7-9 hours daily). A lack of sleep impairs attention, memory and decision-making ability.	Drink alcohol excessively, or every day. Alcohol is a toxin and a depressant. There are many better ways to relax.
Take 20-minute power naps to boost alertness, performance and mood. Between around 1pm and 3pm is ideal, but otherwise, early evening is good too.	Sit or lie around for too long. If your work involves sitting down all day, try and take a walk every day to offset the negative effects of this.
Take breathing breaks to oxygenate your system. Take a deep-ish breath in through your nose (taking the air into your stomach first, then your chest), then let it go through your mouth, as if blowing out a candle. Repeat for a couple of minutes.	Expend too much energy without sufficient rest/recharging time. Be sure to balance your energy expenditure with rest and renewal activity.
Get outside for a moderate dose of daylight (including vitamin D and fresh air) every day where possible.	Smoke. Smoking is said to be the single worst thing we can do for our bodies. Get help to quit if needed.
Avoid or minimise stress. If something costs you your peace of mind, it may also cost you your physical health. Nothing is worth that.	Over-indulge in screen-time. Similarly, avoid excess electromagnetic frequency exposure (EMFs, from X-rays, MRI scans, microwaves, UV light, computers, tablets, mobile phones and phone masts). The W.H.O. has

Do...	Don't...
	said there's a possible link to cancer in some people.
Exercise your brain as well as your body. Keep it busy learning. Teach others what you've learned. Read often. Stimulate your brain with new experiences. Do puzzles and quizzes for stimulation if needed.	Take recreational drugs. They have negative physical and mental side effects, can be addictive/habit forming, and you never really know what's in them.
Have a massage periodically – ideally a professional one with a tailored blend of essential oils.	Drink too much coffee, caffeinated soft drinks, or take caffeine supplements. Caffeine is an addictive stimulant, and more than a few cups a day can cause anxiety, high blood pressure and heart rate, insomnia, muscle breakdown and rebound fatigue.

THE MENTAL ASPECT

The word mental means "relating to the mind." It's just as important to look after the mind as it is the body, because each greatly influences the other.

Often when we talk about the mind, we are really talking about the brain (i.e. the physical apparatus). However, the mind and the brain are two quite separate things, and finding a good and simple explanation of what the mind is, can prove difficult – probably because we're still learning and trying to get our heads around it!

The use of the word 'mind' in this book relates to the non-physical seat of our consciousness and thoughts – the individual small mind that connects to the bigger, collective, universal mind. The mental aspect of an individual incorporates the three elements of mind, consciousness and thought.

Because our thoughts create our reality, looking after our mind involves becoming conscious of the content of our thinking, and identifying any unhelpful thoughts that, left unchecked, could lead to an undesirable effect. We then have the opportunity to examine the validity of these thoughts, and either let them go or replace them with more helpful, constructive thoughts as appropriate.

It's also about becoming more present and conscious in general, so that we don't overdo our thinking. The mind seems to work best when it's relaxed, open, and free from stress. These conditions also enable us to access the deeper levels of insight, wisdom and intelligence from the universal mind.

Activities that support the mind include:

- Mindfulness practice
- Meditation in all its forms
- Creative visualisation
- Creative pursuits of all kinds
- Listening to music
- Therapy, counselling and coaching
- Training in effective/high performance thinking skills
- Training in stress management and/or resilience.

THE EMOTIONAL ASPECT

Life isn't all sunshine and roses for anyone. Sometimes we face problems and challenges. Sometimes it's a lot of hard work. Occasionally, 'bad' things happen in our lives. We probably all experience the full spectrum of emotions in our lifetime and they are all - in their own way - valuable, as they help to guide us towards what's good for us, and away from what isn't.

For the most part, I think we're here to be happy. Our natural state, when we go beyond our thoughts, is one of peace and well-being, but sometimes our thinking gets in the way. When we think of the sky, the sun is always shining up there but some days it's obscured by clouds. The clouds are like the thinking that blocks us from experiencing the sunshine.

We tend to use the words 'emotions' and 'feelings' interchangeably to mean the same thing, although they are really two distinct sides of the same coin. According to neuroscientist Professor Antonio Damasio, emotions are the physical states we experience within our bodies in response to external stimuli, and feelings are our mental experiences of those physical states. With the prospect of a bungee jump over a very high bridge, for example, the body is going to have a strong physical response. Some will experience this as a feeling of extreme excitement... others will experience it as a feeling of sheer dread and panic. For the purposes of this section, 'the emotional aspect' refers to both sides of the coin – our basic emotions and their accompanying feelings.

Emotions and feelings are central to the human experience, and some people appear to be more emotionally sensitive than others. Whilst a highly sensitive nervous system could be perceived as something of a disadvantage, it can also be seen as an advantage, in that the person is so attuned to the world and the people around them that they're literally able to access more emotion-based information (and by association, to resolve more problems and achieve better results) than a less tuned-in person.

This means that emotionally sensitive people experience deeper feelings than those who are less sensitive – a bonus when you consider the 'positive' side of the emotional spectrum, but potentially a disadvantage when you consider the 'negative' side of the spectrum. However, it's how the emotions are perceived and handled that makes the difference between an emotionally intelligent person and an emotionally volatile one.

Emotional intelligence (the capacity for recognising our own feelings and those of others; for motivating ourselves; and for managing emotions effectively in ourselves and others) is one of the most useful sets of skills we can develop. It isn't about learning to control our emotions and feelings so much as it's about learning to fully experience, understand and process them, so that we can learn from them and then let them go.

Whilst in some situations it's appropriate to deal with emotions as they rise, and simply express what wants to come out, in other situations it might be better to simply breathe through them in the moment, 'parking' them temporarily if we can until we're in a safe, nurturing space where we can really open up to them, explore them and allow them to run their course. Personally, I like to do this in the bath (especially if I know that tears are likely), as there's something very comforting about being held and supported by the warm water around you. It can be helpful to put some music on too, although the 'right' kind of music will be subjective, so follow your gut on this.

When you're ready, you would simply need to invite the 'parked' emotions and feelings to re-surface, and allow yourself to be in the moment with them... present and aware, without resistance. Allow your body to respond in whatever way it wants to and stay with the emotions and feelings until they subside. It's interesting to note that even painful feelings carry a kind of beauty within them.

When you've allowed the feelings to run their course, ask yourself whichever of the following reflection questions are relevant to the situation, and be very honest with yourself in your replies:

- What, specifically, have I been feeling?
- What happened today to trigger these feelings? (Stick to the facts)
- What did I say and what did I do?
- What did the other person/people involved say and do?
- How did I interpret what happened?
- What assumptions did I make?
- Might I be deleting, distorting, generalising or making any other thinking errors?
- How else could these events be interpreted?
- Were events today a first, or do they reflect a pattern? If so, what's the common theme (i.e. what is the key thought or belief) present in these events?
- When I hold this thought or belief up to scrutiny, is it true? (if in doubt, ask a friend)

- Is there anything I could have done differently that would have got a better response or outcome?
- What's good, useful or beautiful about this situation?
- What have I learned?
- Are there any actions I need to take in order to address this situation?

Some people like to write things down in a journal or notebook. Some prefer to talk them through with a friend, coach or therapist. Some prefer to just think them through. Whichever you choose, you should notice that you feel much better/lighter afterwards. Feel good about yourself for courageously facing your feelings, and then move on.

Here are a few more things you can do to support your emotions:

- Aim to do something every day that brings you at least a little bit of joy
- Make time every day for activities that take you out of your thinking mind, so that you can access your natural state of well-being, peace and love. Creative pursuits are great because they tend to bring us back into our bodies – drawing us into sensory experience instead
- Social connection is important. Reach out to your friends and family when you need emotional support. We all need other people and our relationships can be a significant source of help and happiness
- Be selective about who you spend time with and consider the balance of give and take in your relationships. Avoid negative people who drain your energy and put you down,

and seek out those who radiate positive energy and build you up

- If you have a worry or concern, talk things through in confidence with a person who has been trained to listen objectively and non-judgementally. Some workplaces provide free, confidential employee assistance helplines, and Samaritans in the UK provides free support to anyone in emotional distress, 24/7/365

- Check out natural remedies that support the emotions, such as supplements, tea infusions, essential oils and herbal/flower remedies

- Use music therapy to support you – whether you need to feel calm, uplifted, happy, energised, or otherwise

- Read books and/or attend training courses about emotional intelligence, and seek to develop your skills around the themes of self-awareness, self-management, social awareness and relationship management

- You may wish to check out some of the healing modalities said to help balance or heal the emotions, including Reiki, Emotional Freedom Technique (EFT), Vibrational Medicine, Crystal Healing, Sound Healing, EMF Balancing Technique, and others. I cannot vouch for all these modalities personally, but would invite you to do your own research and investigate any that resonate with you.

THE SPIRITUAL ASPECT

This aspect is harder to understand and describe than the

physical, mental and emotional aspects, but is our inner spirit or soul essence... the non-physical 'being' that resides within our physical bodies and is who we really are. All religions, and most people, seem to acknowledge this aspect of life even though, to date, it hasn't been scientifically proven. We just seem to have a sense of 'knowing' that it's real.

It can be easy to overlook our spiritual nature, as we can't see it, hear it or touch it, however it's arguably just as important (and possibly even more so) than the other three aspects of ourselves, because it's our very essence – the part of us that is said to live on long after our bodies, thoughts and emotions have gone.

Honouring and nurturing the essence of who we really are is essential to our happiness and well-being. Here are some activities that can enable us to do that:

- Spending some quiet time alone in meditation
- Spending time out in nature – on a beach, in a forest, up a mountain, by a lake, etc
- Doing some gardening, nurturing plants and flowers and growing our own food
- Finding a bit of time each week (or each day, ideally) to do something our spirit truly loves
- Expressing our spirit creatively through art, music, poetry, writing or any creative hobby
- Expressing our spirit creatively though our clothes, home, and so on
- Connecting with other good souls and enjoying quality time together

- Doing things for other people, for the love of helping and giving
- Visiting the places we've always had an inner longing to visit
- Doing the things we've always had an inner longing to do
- Reading good, spiritual material
- Sending love and forgiveness to those that have hurt us, as best we can
- If we're religious, praying, singing, chanting, going to our place of worship, and so on

The activities listed within each of the four sections here, all benefit the other three aspects, and are therefore interchangeable. They will all support you in maintaining the clarity and quality of your thinking, and in becoming happier and healthier all-round. However, balance is important, and we can overdo or underdo activity in any of these areas.

I believe that feeling good is one of our most important jobs in life, and that we should make our happiness a priority. When we feel good, we lift everyone around us up too, and when we feel good, we attract and create more good in our lives too. However, that means that we need to proactively build some fun and joy into our lives to ensure that our needs in this area are met.

Take some time now to reflect on the activities that you can build into your life that would have the most benefit to your health and happiness, and make some notes on the following pages:

Physical Aspect:

Do What?	By When?	Notes...

Mental Aspect:

Do What?	By When?	Notes...

Emotional Aspect:

Do What?	By When?	Notes...

Spiritual Aspect:

Do What?	By When?	Notes...

CHAPTER 8 SUMMARY

✓ Looking after our thinking equipment doesn't just mean looking after our brain. Our heart and gut are also centres of intelligence in the body

✓ Each aspect of ourselves (physical, mental, emotional and spiritual) affects the others, hence we need to take a holistic approach for the best results, engaging in some nurturing activity in each area

✓ Balance is important. We shouldn't overdo or underdo the time we spend nurturing any one aspect

✓ Our happiness and well-being are in our own hands, and it's important to have a bit of fun and find a bit of joy along the way. If we're not filling our own glass up, we won't have much to share with others

✓ The benefits are that we won't just improve how we think – we will also improve how we look, how we feel and how we operate. The outcome will be a happier, healthier, more successful version of ourselves, enabling us to get better results and increase our prosperity.

"CHANGE YOUR THOUGHTS
AND YOU CAN CHANGE
YOUR WORLD"

- NORMAN VINCENT
PEALE -

Chapter 9

SEEING THE BIGGER PICTURE

This book has described how you can transform any area of your life, and make your goals and dreams come true, by changing how you think, which changes how you feel and what you do. That may well be all that you need, but before this book is through, I'd also like to point out the potential to influence wider change, should you be that way inclined.

When we change our thinking in some way, we will almost certainly be impacting and influencing others without even knowing it. This is because we're influenced by one another's energy fields, and connected at the level of the superconscious mind. When we change our outlook or attitude, for example, it extends a compelling invitation to those we're dealing with to change theirs too (although they're free to choose not to, if they don't want to).

Whilst we can't, and shouldn't try to, directly change other people or control what they do, we can often influence them through our own example, and by providing the kind of information, stories and interventions that might make them want to change (and make it easy for them). I should add that the only time it would be ethical to do so is when the change would be for their own benefit (for example, influencing behaviour change that would benefit their health), or where there's a 'greater good' at stake, like climate change, for example. Otherwise it would be a violation of free will, and would either not work, backfire or come at a high cost (and not financially).

The Sunshine Method described in this book, can also be applied to people-related change and improvement opportunities locally, nationally and even globally. Any dissatisfactory situation that's being caused or influenced by how people are thinking, feeling or what they're doing can be improved by using this process.

When we look around us, we can probably all see things that would benefit from transformation. Often, it's the larger systems and institutions - financial, political/governmental, religious, judicial, educational, welfare, healthcare, media, and so on. Then there are industries like food, manufacturing, chemical, clothing and energy. Many large organisations (and some small and medium sized ones too) are obsessed with growth and increasing profits above all else, when that's not always sustainable. Often, it's culture that needs to change first - the ideas, customs and behaviours of an organisation, group or society – then, the more obvious, tangible changes can follow.

Too often we steer clear of trying to influence these things because they feel too big and overwhelming. Maybe we don't believe they can ever change. Often, we wish somebody would do something about them, forgetting that we are somebody! Individually, we are limited in our influence, however, collectively we hold more power than we realise. Collectively we can change the world! The difficulty is that we are not always united. We focus on our differences, forgetting that, at the higher level, we all have the same needs and want the same things (love, peace, fulfilment, health, happiness, and so on). When we work together with a shared purpose, we can achieve anything; however, our beliefs are self-fulfilling... if we believe we can bring about change, we will make it happen; if we believe we can't, we won't even try.

Of course, change isn't always easy, and it often meets with resistance. You will need to make it as easy and safe for people as possible, clearly communicating why it's necessary, how it will benefit them and how they can take full advantage of the opportunities. You will also need a compelling vision and an excellent project plan, along with a great team and some contingencies for the unexpected.

I recommend checking out the book, *Influencer – The New Science of Leading Change* (Joseph Grenny et al – McGraw Hill) to anyone serious about achieving larger-scale behaviour change. If possible, attend the 'Influencer' training course (for information, go to www.vitalsmarts.com). There's also a collection of free, change-related microlearning available on mobile learning platform SmartUp's 'Changemakers' community. From a smartphone or tablet, download the 'SmartUp Learn' app from the App Store. Enter the community name 'changemakers' in the blank field: _____.smartup.io, and sign-up.

As individuals, we are at the centre of our experience, however, we are not at the centre of the universe, and nor do all things revolve around us – even if it feels like they do! As much as we have physical individuality and our own personality, we are, in fact, only a small part of a greater collective, interdependent on one other, much like cells in the human body are. Each cell has a different job to do but whatever happens in one part of the body can have a negative impact on the other parts, with the effect of disease or dysfunction taking a lot of the available energy and resource away from the whole. Similarly, we're all affected by what's happening elsewhere in the world, even if we don't consciously feel it, and other parts of the world are affected by what's happening here. In some cases, the things that are happening are a potential threat to our collective existence, and we need to wake up to the threats and start acting.

Not everyone will want to lead change, but everyone can play a part in making it happen. The question is, "What are the things that you care passionately about (or that bother you), that you would love to play a part in protecting or improving?"

It's said that "charity begins at home" - that our first responsibility is to ourselves, our families and friends – and maybe that's true. However, it's probably also true that we're here in service of something bigger – of the collective – and we will all feel inspired to make a difference in different ways, and to different things. For example, you might have a leaning towards benefiting the environment, or animals, or something connected with wealth or poverty, housing, equality, food, water, government, spirituality, justice, education or well-being.

At different stages in our lives we will have more or less time and energy to give to these matters. If you have the capacity currently, give some thought to what change initiative(s) you could start or perhaps help with, that relates to the things you care about. Even if you only gently questioned or challenged faulty and/or unhelpful beliefs, that would be a significant contribution.

Imagine for a moment how the world would change if most of us did the following:

- viewed everyone as important
- treated ourselves and others with love and compassion
- were emotionally honest with each another, in a kind and respectful way
- listened deeply to each other without judgement, in order to learn and understand
- consumed only what we needed
- made decisions that represented the best interests of all concerned
- took responsibility for nurturing and prospering ourselves, other people, our planet, and all its life forms.

What kind of outcomes do you think we would see? What improvements would there be in areas such as conflict and war, health and well-being, environment and climate change, poverty and hunger, education, and so on? Would the issues here even continue to exist?

Some people scoff at the idea of a world where people conduct themselves with this level of consciousness, integrity and responsibility, saying that it's utopian and unrealistic. However, whilst the world will probably never be 'perfect' as we understand it, it would seem to me that these actions are not outside of the bounds of human capability. When you look at these actions, there's nothing that isn't teachable or learnable.

Whilst we might never have a situation where everyone behaves in this way (it is a planet of free will and choice after all, and not everyone will see the benefits), it's reasonable to believe that the greater majority of people could be raised or taught to operate as such. Again – we need to be conscious of our beliefs about what is and isn't possible, because they will tend to be self-fulfilling.

For this reason, I believe we need to hold a vision of the highest potential for humankind, modelling and promoting these actions, and ignoring the naysayers who say it's impossible. As the Chinese proverb tells us: "The person who says it cannot be done should not interrupt the person who is doing it!"

Anthropologist Margaret Mead once famously said: "Never doubt that a small group of thoughtful, committed citizens can change the world. Indeed, it's the only thing that ever has." So, I hope you'll join me in dreaming big – both in your own personal lives, and in your visions for the bigger picture. I believe we can create and achieve whatever we put our hearts and minds to, if we drop our fearful and limited thinking, and allow our love and passion for the important things that we care about to shine through. In fact, the power of love trumps even the power of thought in its capacity for transformation, but that's a whole other book!

All power to you, and may your passion be mightier than your Kryptonite!

"ENDINGS ARE BEGINNINGS, AND BEGINNINGS ARE OURS TO TURN INTO SOMETHING GOOD"

- ELIZABETH CHANDLER -

Martine's Story

My thinking hasn't always been my superpower! I have probably been guilty of most of the thinking errors detailed in this book, at some time or another, and to be honest, I can still catch myself going down the path of worry, fear and doubt at times. The difference is that these days, I catch and redirect myself much earlier.

I had quite an unsettled and difficult early life, experiencing a twice-broken home, multiple house moves, homelessness and relative deprivation. We were a one-parent family for much of the time, living in social housing and on benefits. I grew up lacking in confidence and with limited life and social skills, feeling that I wasn't as good as other people.

In my mid-to-late teens I developed an eating disorder that consumed me for about 7 years. My thinking - along with my moods and eating habits - was all over the place. I felt so terrible most of the time, that I wonder now how I managed to drag myself through those days!

After leaving home at 17, I jumped from job to job and place to place – never really feeling settled, or like I belonged. A few years later I discovered 'self-help', and later, was fortunate to find my way to some excellent training and bits of therapy that helped me to get myself and my life on track.

Eventually I met my husband, and went on to have two children. Having a family has anchored me, and helped me to become a happier, healthier, more grounded kind of person.

In my 30s, I found my passion in corporate training and coaching, soaking up every bit of useful information that I could. What I learned was so useful and transformational to me, that it was a joy to share it with others. I also trained in neuro-linguistic programming (NLP) and hypnotherapy during this time, as I wanted to help people at a deeper, more personal level than was sometimes possible in the group training environment.

The understanding that every result in life and in business is traceable back to the quality of thinking taking place, led to the design of my 'Sunshine Method' model, and in 2018 I went into business with the aim of helping as many people and organisations as possible transform their results, and become happier, healthier, more successful and more prosperous.

It's still relatively early days, and the business and myself are a work in progress! My goals are big enough to scare me a little, but I'm enjoying the process and taking things one step at a time.

I know people who were brought up in the care system, who've been in prison and addicted to drink and drugs, who've turned their lives around and made a success of themselves. I'm pretty sure that if they can do that, there's hope for everyone.

My very best wishes as you work to make changes in your life.

Acknowledgements

I am massively grateful to everyone who's had an input into helping me write this book.

To my immediate family for their love and support – to Edd, my lovely husband of nearly 25 years and our two gorgeous boys Joe and Max for largely getting on with life whilst I holed myself away in the office writing for hours on end, sometimes forgetting when it was dinner time and occasionally forgetting to smile and be welcoming when they would wander in for a chat and my attention was deep into something else!

To Karen Williams and Sheryl Andrews of Librotas Book Mentoring & Publishing for helping me to get started, and for their advice and encouragement at the Author's Journey networking events they run.

To Jane Cooke and my 'Free Range Women in Business' sisters for their friendship, love and support over the last 18 months. A mighty host of angels, if ever there was one!

To David White and Nick Haverly who took time and energy out of their busy lives to read the book and give me quality feedback that resulted in a better end product.

To illustrator and graphic recorder extraordinaire Emma Paxton, who fabulously turned my half-baked ideas into charming illustrations which have brought extra personality, quirkiness and appeal. Thank you, Emma, for your patience and good humour throughout.

And finally, to Lyn and Paul Thurman at The Quiet Rebel Bureau, who took my very basic manuscript, and magicked it into a real book! Thank you for your help and encouragement in getting my work out into the world ☺.

For details of corporate and public workshops, events and retreats on the theme of 'Your Thinking is Your Superpower' (and other subjects), visit www.sunshinedevelopment.co.uk.

Printed in Poland
by Amazon Fulfillment
Poland Sp. z o.o., Wrocław

50085648R00159